Brothers in War

GINGER RODEGHERO

Book Cover Design: AuthorPackages

ISBN-13: 978-0960008100 (Paperback)

DISCLAIMER

This book is designed to provide information on human rights only. This information is provided and sold with the knowledge that the publisher and author do not offer any legal or medical advice. In the case of a need for any such expertise consult with the appropriate professional. This book does not contain all information available on the subject. This book has not been created to be specific to any individual people or organization's situation or needs. Reasonable efforts have been made to make this book as accurate as possible. However, there may be typographical and or content errors. Therefore, this book should serve only as a general guide. This book contains information that might be dated or erroneous and is intended only to educate and entertain. The author and publisher shall have no liability or responsibility to any person or entity regarding any loss or damage incurred, or alleged to have incurred, directly or indirectly, by the information contained in this book or as a result of anyone acting or failing to act upon the information in this book. You hereby agree never to sue and to hold the author and publisher harmless from any and all claims arising out of the information contained in this book. You hereby agree to be bound by this disclaimer, covenant not to sue and release. You may return this book within the guaranteed time period for a full refund. In the interest of full disclosure, this book may contain affiliate links that might pay the author or publisher a commission upon any purchase from the company. While the author and publisher take no responsibility for any virus or technical issues that could be caused by such links, the business practices of these companies and/or the performance of any product or service, the author or publisher have used the product or service and make a recommendation in good faith based on that experience. All characters are fictitious. Any resemblance to other real persons, living or dead, is purely coincidental. The opinions and stories in this book are the views of the authors and not those of the publisher.

DEDICATION

To Josh and Ayva

CONTENTS

ACKNOWLEDGMENTS

Thank you to Richter Publishing for working with me to disseminate my story; it is a tale that needs to be heard.

INTRODUCTION

I am passionate about Human Rights and eliminating the violations of individual rights that still exist in our world today. I feel through knowledge one is able to make change. I hope this story inspires you to make changes in the world around you by arming you with the truth about your Human Rights.

CHAPTER 1

Brett Chance stared out his bedroom window trying to make a simple decision. He hadn't been able to put two thoughts together for the past three weeks. He felt like he was drifting in a nebula and knew he needed to snap out of it. What to do?

It was a crisp Saturday afternoon and Madison, his girlfriend of two years, had sent a text asking him to hang out at the stable while she slopped stalls. Horse people, he thought, they're an interesting breed. To Brett they were obsessive; to Madison it was a passion.

Brett hadn't been to the stable since his world had turned upside down. He weighed his options. Mom had been telling him for days that he needed to get out of the house. The stable is always busy, most people mind their business, and it will probably be safe, he thought.

Besides, I need a break from staring out this window. Sighing, he realized a guy doesn't have much of a choice when two women gang up on him.

Wandering into the kitchen, he grabbed his keys. "Later, Mom!"

"Yeah?" Brett could tell she was trying to sound normal.

"Just heading over to the stables for a bit." Planting a peck on her cheek he headed out the door.

The sunshine of the Indian summer afternoon cast long shadows on the oak-lined lane leading to Lehman Farms near Pittsford, NY. Madison had been boarding Midnight, her three-year-old Arabian, at their stable for the past year. Brett pulled his blue 2001 Mustang into an empty parking space. Brushing back his dark hair he checked himself in the rear-view mirror then unfolded his tall, muscular body from the bucket seat.

Dressed in gym shorts and a Manchester United t-shirt he wound his way past the busy outdoor riding ring and headed for the stables. He inhaled deeply as he stepped inside the long row of stalls. Brett had gotten used to the distinct smell of the barn. Closing his eyes for a moment, he almost felt normal. The smell of the knotty pine boards mixing with alfalfa and mulch created a pleasant scent. He didn't think his mom would ever buy a Yankee Candle named Barn Musk, but the aroma had grown on him.

Horses bobbed their heads in and out of their homes as if they were greeting him. Some slowly munched on hay piled in the troughs outside their doors. Leather harnesses hung here and there from hooks suspended next to each stall. Brett sidestepped a young redhead dressed in knee high riding boots leading her thoroughbred to the indoor riding ring. A wheel barrel piled with manure was parked outside another stall. Brett ducked as a full pitchfork swung his direction. A running hose stuck in a watering bucket was overflowing. As Brett reached down to turn off the spigot, Bruno, the barn mascot raced over to him, his tail going as fast as a wind-up toy.

"I missed you too." Brett stroked the chocolate Lab's smooth coat. He got a sloppy kiss as pay.

He recognized most of the horse people but didn't stop to talk. Brett had no desire to start a conversation that might require him to explain where he'd been the past few weeks. He found Madison outside Midnight's stall. Her tan, muscular legs sprouted from her blue muck boots. Sweat rolled down her back, drenching the Allendale Soccer t-shirt that bore Brett's number 25. Her blond ponytail tick-tocked as she stroked Midnight's shining coat.

Brett softly tapped her on the shoulder. Madison startled. Focused on combing Midnight's mane, she hadn't noticed Brett's arrival. Her face lit up. Stretching on her tiptoes, she brushed his cheek with a soft kiss.

3

He blushed.

"I'm glad you decided to come." She tucked a stray hair behind her studded ear.

"I have to keep the ladies in my life happy." The words caught in his throat and he stopped to compose himself.

Wanting to keep things light Madison put the lid down on her tack box.

"Have a seat." One eye on Brett, she continued brushing Midnight. Halting for an instant she gave him a hesitant smile.

"It's really good to see you, I missed you," he uttered as he stared into her blue eyes. Brett realized that he loved her best like this; sweating, hair a mess, not a care in the world about her appearance, deeply intent on her passion. She'll be a great vet someday he thought as he planted himself on the lid of the box.

Within minutes the rhythm of her dandy brush put Brett into a trance, oblivious to the beehive of the stable activity. Madison's chatter knocked at the edge of his brain.

"So, what do you think Brett? ... BRETT?" His body jolted and his blue eyes came back from the world he was lost in. Madison realized he'd not heard a word she had said.

4

"What's happening? I thought you came to talk."

"Not sure what's happening. I...I just needed to get out of the house," Brett shrugged, trying to orient himself. "I'm not sure where I was."

"Well, wherever you were, it wasn't here." Before he could reply she grabbed his hand and hopped up next to him. Slipping off her boots she cuddled up against Brett's shoulder.

"You know, this is your last year at Allendale." She started slowly, "I don't want you to miss out on the perks of being a senior. You should try to get back to normal."

"I'm just not sure if life will ever be normal again." Brett sounded dismal. Deep down he was wondering if anyone would ever understand how he felt. Growing up, Brett and Jessica, his sister, had always had each other's back. He struggled to sort out how he

could've prevented her death. What should he have said? What should he have done differently? He felt like he had let Jess down.

"Look, I think Jessica would want you to get back to your life."

"How do you know what Jessica would want?" Brett barked. Immediately he regretted that he had lashed out.

"Well, we were friends since junior high. I think I knew her pretty well." Madison's eyebrows folded into a scowl.

"Yeah, well I knew her all my life!" Putting a clamp on his temper, Brett jumped off his perch and headed toward the stall door. I don't want to hurt her feelings he thought.

"Wait, Brett wait," pleaded Madison rushing after him. She gently grabbed his hand. "I'm just saying you need to get back to your life, you have soccer, your scholarship dreams. There's so much ahead of you."

"Well, Jessica has nothing ahead of her." He felt hot tears running down his cheeks. Maybe it wasn't such a great idea to have come here he thought.

He quickly turned and ran headlong into Mr. Lehman, the stable owner. Mr. Lehman ran a tight ship and didn't take kindly to anyone disturbing the peace.

"You kids alright?" His eyes darted between Madison and Brett like a humming bird searching for food. A piercing stare landed on Brett.

"Yeah, we're good, Mr. Lehman," Madison tried to sound cheerful. Staring at Brett, her eyes begged for his cooperation. She didn't need to be on Mr. Lehman's bad list.

"Well remember, no disturbing the other boarders,"

his eyes were locked on Brett.

Brett's timid nod broke the hold of Mr. Lehman's grimace. Without another word, the old man moseyed down the lane, his boots scraping the cobblestone.

Picking at the bristles of her dandy brush, Madison could feel Brett's pain but didn't know what to say to ease his anguish.

"Coach Bronson asked me how you were doing." She was grabbing at straws.

The comment peaked Brett's interest. "What did you tell him?"

"Nothing really, just that you were going to be back soon, the team needs you, ya know." She clung to the small change in his tone that she'd heard.

"Yeah, yeah, I'll think about it." He almost meant it.

Despite the fact that he didn't sound certain, Madison persisted. "How about Monday, just come to class and see how it goes. It's the first step back to normal."

"I'll think about it." His softer reply gave Madison a twinge of hope.

Together they headed through the stalls toward the entrance, oblivious to the others around them. Madison felt an electrical charge between them, fueled by Brett's silence. Reaching the end of the hall, Brett turned and walked away.

"Hey," Madison called, but Brett ambled on out the door.

Head down, shoulders slumped Brett skirted across the barnyard heading for his car trying to avoid crossing paths with any horse people. He usually blew Madison a kiss as he drove away, not tonight.

Heart broken, Madison headed back toward Midnight's stall. She still had work to do before putting the Arabian to bed. Tidying up and securing her tack box she replayed the conversation back and forth like a tape player on rewind. *What should I have said to make Brett feel better? I know he's hurting, I want to help him, but this is uncharted territory for me too. Maybe he doesn't realize how this has affected everyone who knew Jess.*

Going through her normal lock-up routine, she double-checked the stall latch. Giving Midnight a final treat from her pocket, Madison headed to her car. Saying her good-byes to the few people hanging out, she shot a quick text to Brett, *"See you Monday ☺, Maddie!"*

She didn't get a reply.

#####

Pulling into the parking lot at Allendale Columbia Campus on Monday morning, Brett quickly found a vacant spot reserved for seniors. His sweaty palms made the steering wheel slick and his breakfast threatened to revisit. Closing his eyes and lying

his head back he recited a litany to himself. "Just open the door, just open the door, just open the door." He knew once he got out of the car he was committed.

The engine still idling, he reached for the keys and found the courage to turn the car off. "Alright, just one step at a time...it's still early...not many people here yet." He searched for any encouraging thought he could cook up. He dragged himself from the seat of the car, clicked the key fob and headed across the courtyard.

The four colonial style buildings surrounding the commons had yet to awaken. When the six hundred students of Allendale converged on the grounds there would be organized chaos until the morning bells chimed. Scouting the grounds for fellow students Brett noticed the birch trees that outlined the perimeter of the campus. Awed by the rainbow of changing colors, he realized that everything eventually dies.

Brett slipped into American Government class five minutes before the bell. He headed straight for an empty desk in the back and slid into the seat, avoiding eye contact with the few kids meandering around. The last thing Brett wanted was to answer that inevitable question, "how you are doing?" Trying to be invisible, he was sure the whispers in the room were about him.

Brett jumped when Madison touched his sleeve. "Jeez, don't sneak up on a person." A huddle of fellow students glanced his way.

"Sorry. I'm glad you took my advice, just act normal." She dropped her books on the desktop and plopped into the seat beside him.

"You keep saying that," he murmured. The room was beginning to buzz as more kids showed up for class. Brett kept his head down hoping to avoid any eye contact that could solicit a conversation.

She shrugged. "Still, glad you're here." Madison lazily crossed her legs and tapped her boot against Brett's chair. Finally getting his attention, she flashed her best smile. She hoped to infect him with a positive vibe. It didn't work. Brett slumped deeper into his chair.

The bell rang as Ms. Michaels walked in, directing a new student to the empty seat in front of her. Something about him set off an alarm in Brett's brain.

Ms. Michaels stopped in her tracks as she set her planner on the desk. She gave Brett a genuine smile, "Great to see you."

Please, please, please don't ask me, was running through his head. Please no questions about Jess. He held his breathe; waiting to be put on center stage, but Ms. Michael's attention turned to the dark skinned, wiry student seated in front of her.

Sounding like a tire with a leak, Brett slowly exhaled. Staring at him, Madison's face was punctuated with a question mark.

"What?" He threw her way. "Saved by the new kid!"

After a brief clamor of chairs, everyone settled into their seats. Kids liked American Government for the most part. Ms. Michael's enthusiasm about her subject and her style of teaching expanded their viewpoints. Everyone was given an opportunity to express their opinion with no judgment attached. Posted over the white board was her favorite saying, "You guys are the future, it will be good or bad depending upon what you make it." Ms. Michaels made a difference and students respected her.

She stepped to the podium in the center of the room. "I would like to introduce a new student, Rasheed Poya. Is the pronunciation correct?" She had directed her question to the new guy.

"Yes, Madam." The strong accent perked Brett's curiosity but there was no need to try and figure out where he was from.

Ms. Michaels to the rescue. "Rasheed is from Afghanistan."

Brett felt like a bomb went off in his stomach. His eyes drilled a hole in the back of Rasheed's head. He needed to get a good look at this guy. Knowing Ms. Michaels, Brett sensed they were in for a long discussion about Rasheed's world.

"What brought you to America, is your family here Rasheed?" The questions began.

"No Madam, my family is still in Afghanistan, I am living with my aunt." His speech sounded very formal and very British.

"Hey, how'd you learn English?" A student up front posed the obvious question.

Hesitantly, he explained, "My parents went to University in England, they taught English to my sister and I. My father believes it is the language of commerce."

"Well, welcome." Ms. Michaels offered her hand and Rasheed bobbed his head in a respectful bow. "We would love to hear about your country. What does your father do?"

The war in Brett's stomach escalated. He did not want to even hear the word "Afghanistan" much less find out what life was like there. But this was the kind of stuff Ms. Michaels loved and the class knew it would distract her from the day's lesson.

Rasheed relaxed a bit. He was soon going on about his dad working on some hydroelectric dam. His dad was the head engineer and Rasheed acted like he was the most important man on the job. His family lived in the capitol of the Helmand Province, near the dam. The dam had been damaged during attacks in 2001 and then again in 2007 by the Taliban. His father was responsible to get it running again.

Before long the students were barraging Rasheed with questions. Laying his head on the desk, Brett tried to tune out the soundtrack that fueled his stomach's turmoil. Of course, Ms. Michaels encouraged the lively conversation about Afghan trivia. But then she asked the mega-question, "Rasheed, were you ever in danger because of the war?"

Catapulting from his seat, Brett's desk toppled over.

"What the...!" Brett stopped midsentence. He knew first-hand about the dangers in Afghanistan. There was a full-blown battle going on inside him now, the last bombing run exploding in his stomach.

"Brett!" Madison tried to contain her shock and calm his outburst.

"Yeah, are you siding with the Afghan?" Brett's eyes drilled through her.

"I'm not siding." She gestured air-quotes around the last word.

Brett knew he had screwed up coming to school today. What were the odds this Afghan would show up the day he had mustered the courage to come back to school?

"Enough!" Brett's outburst produced a stunned silence in the room.

All eyes were definitely on him now. This was not acceptable behavior at Allendale and very out of character for Brett. Before Ms. Michaels could address the transgression, Brett bolted from the class leaving his book bag behind. Picking it up Madison raced after him leaving Ms. Michaels trying to bring order to the ensuing ruckus.

"What was that all about?" Madison chased him down and grabbed his arm.

"You don't understand!" With a sneer, he pulled away.

"Try me," she searched his face.

Scanning for some kind of an explanation, Brett drew a blank. How could he give her an answer when he didn't understand the feelings that were boiling inside? Glaring at her he snatched the bag and raced for the exit.

Madison was shell-shocked, how could she help him when he wasn't willing to be helped. Frozen like a statue, she wondered if she should go after him. What would she say? This was not the Brett she knew.

Blinded by tears, Brett raced across the commons and ran headlong into Coach Bronson. He stopped short, surprised to be eye to eye with his soccer coach. Not knowing what to do, he murmured an apology and dashed off.

"Hey Brett!" Coach called after him but Brett put his head down and darted toward his car.

He jumped into his Mustang and squealed the tires racing out of the parking lot. Normally that would earn the guilty party a detention but Brett didn't intend to be back at school anytime soon.

CHAPTER 2

Brett found himself sitting on the old stone staircase next to the train tunnel at Corbett's Glen. He wasn't quite sure how he'd arrived here after the drama at school, ignoring his coach and speeding out of the parking lot.

He did know why he'd ended up next to Tunnel Falls. This was his place. His best childhood memories were of the many visits he'd made to Corbett's Glen with his Sicilian grandfather.

Flipping stones into the sparkling waterfalls, he'd finally calmed his racing heart. He closed his eyes and listened for the symphony in the rushing water; pounding drums, dancing flutes, a merry fiddle. Gramps said you could hear them all if you took heed.

He pulled a tattered, folded picture of his grandfather from his wallet, taken at this exact spot when he was only six. Studying his grandfather's smile, he felt like he was looking in a mirror. He shared the same cowlick on his forehead, and though his grandfather's hair was gray, he knew his own dark, wavy locks were a trait he'd inherited from Gramps. People said he was a mini version of this old man in more ways than his appearance.

Brett always looked forward to outings at the park with Gramps. They walked Goldie, the family retriever, explored the trails, and on warm days often waded in the clear, sparkling water. But mostly they talked. Gramps always shared his "pearls" as he called them. It was those man-to-man talks that had shaped so much of Brett's attitude about life. And Gramps loved to rehash Brett's soccer games! He had never missed any of Brett's games, up until the day he had his heart attack.

Brett got up and stretched his long limbs. Tucking the picture safely in his wallet, he headed toward the north trails. Being Monday morning, the park was not busy and Brett enjoyed the solitude of the woods. A striped chipmunk scampered up an ancient oak. Brett inhaled deeply and took in the smell of the moss and fresh cut grass. The sights and smells of the nature preserve elicited fond memories.

Brett pondered the wisdom his grandfather had shared with him over the years. When he was young the conversations were more about getting along with his sister and helping his mom. But as he grew older the chats focused more on the meaning of life. Maybe I should've recorded some of those talks thought Brett. I could use some of those "pearls" right now.

He headed down the north trail kicking at the woodchips and soon found himself at the Seating Stones. Brett eased himself onto the old, worn stone shaped like a seat from years of people finding repose there. Rubbing the smooth sandstone, he recalled a particular exchange he'd had with his grandfather not long before he died. They were sitting on the exact same spot having a heart to heart.

They'd been talking about Brett's game from the night before, his team had been crushed. Brett hadn't been pleased with his performance and was giving Gramps a play-by-play of all the things he'd screwed up. His grandfather had stopped him mid-sentence and asked him for one thing he'd done right.

Pondering for a moment, Brett recalled a run that he had made toward the end of the game. He'd carried the ball up the right field, beating three opponents with some fancy footwork and served a perfect cross. Too bad though, Nelson had missed the finish and the team remained scoreless.

Gramps backed him up to the perfect cross. "Envisioning what you want to happen will bring it to fruition." That was definitely one of Gramps' best "pearls". Brett had used that one before every game since and more times than not it had worked.

Brett got up and wandered on down the open trail. The air was crisp and clear. Fall was beckoning; it had always been Gramps' favorite time of the year.

Gosh, Brett wondered, what pearl would Gramps have shared after the scene he'd created this morning? He definitely would have been "troubled with my behavior," he thought. As a youngster, whenever Gramps said that to Brett, he'd known that he'd disappointed his grandfather. "Compose yourself," he'd say with a stern look. Those words always cued Brett that he was out of line. Seemed like good advice today!

Brett noticed a squirrel nearby, packing his cheeks with a winter stash. Gramps frequently used the examples of nature to impart his wisdom to Brett. He'd explained how the little squirrel worked tirelessly to prepare for his future. His success and survival depended entirely on his dedication to his job.

That little anecdote had been shared on a day when Brett was grumbling about how hard the coach had been pushing the team. Brett never bellyached about hard work again.

He stopped short—maybe Maddie was right. The realization came like a breath of fresh air. He had work to do to prepare for his future. Putting his attention on his scholarship goals just might be the diversion his mind needed.

Turning for his car he made a new resolve to be the best soccer player he could be. Hard work! That's the drill! He pulled left out of the park onto Penfield Road heading back toward school.

Brett pulled slowly into the lot he'd blazed out of just a few hours earlier.

Surprisingly, the spot he'd vacated was still available. Glancing at his watch he knew it was time to head to the cafeteria.

The din of the lunchroom assured him that everyone's attention was on their food and conversations. He made a beeline to the table in the corner that he always shared with his friends. When he plopped down next to Madison, her startled expression told him that she hadn't expected to see him back here today. She was clearly trying to figure out what to say, but Brett beat her to the punch.

"Thanks," he whispered.

"For what?" Her bewildered look confirmed that his behavior had her in complete confusion.

"Just for caring. For being you." Brett flashed the smile he had seen in the picture of Gramps.

As the afternoon ticked by, Brett kept his focus on the upcoming soccer practice and his new resolve. He managed to make it through the rest of his classes without replaying any of the morning's drama. He'd pushed aside all thoughts of the Afghan. Fortunately, the new kid hadn't turned up in any of Brett's afternoon classes, helping him to stay composed.

At the final bell, he gathered the books he needed for homework from his locker. Feeling a twinge of excitement, he headed to the practice field with his soccer bag slung across his shoulder. It will be good to get back on the field he thought. His phone buzzed interrupting his anticipation.

A text from Maddie, "Hey where are you, I need to talk to you?"

He shot a quick response; "I'm headed to soccer, later."

The campus sports complex was a buzz of activity. The cross-country team was limbering up, heading for their run through the birch-lined nature trails. The lady varsity tennis players were chattering among themselves as they loaded on the school's bus, excited about the coming match with Naples High. There was always something going on at Allendale.

His phone vibrated again as he darted past the activity and across the open field, but Brett ignored the text. He'd spotted a single player on the sidelines juggling a ball in a manner he'd never seen before. Who was that? He didn't know anyone on the Wolves varsity team that could handle a ball with such finesse. A few steps more and a feeling of dread crept in...was that Rasheed?

Oh geez, what is he doing here? Brett's earlier resolve melted as quickly as ice on a hot summer day, triggering a puddle of emotion. Glancing at his phone he saw that Maddie had been trying to alert him, Rasheed plays soccer.

He closed his eyes for a moment and tried to compose himself. Ok, Gramps he thought. Taking a deep breath, he stashed his phone in the end pouch of his soccer bag, grabbed his ball and joined the rest of the team in their warm-up stretches and ball touches. Brett kept an eagle eye on every move the new kid made.

Coach Bronson whistled the team together. He caught Brett's eye. Brett wanted to somehow reassure his coach that he'd be fine.

Coach Bronson split the team up and gave them instructions regarding the 3-on-3, give and go drills they would be doing. Brett was squared up against Rasheed. The drill was not going well for him. Every time Brett had the ball, Rasheed managed to make the right move and intercept the pass before it reached the target player. Every time Rasheed had the ball, he managed to blow past Brett. Brett continually got sucked into making his first move in the wrong direction.

Shaking his head and wiping the sweat from his brow, Brett felt his frustration building. He didn't understand what was going on in his head. He was always the guy that picked up the fallen opponent. The player that always gave the high fives and encouraged the other man, but now he felt an anger growing inside him. It was about to erupt and he wasn't sure how to deal with it.

Brett saw Coach Bronson moving between the small groups spread across the practice field. As the coach approached his group, Brett felt his tension over Rasheed hitting max overload.

"What's up Brett?"

"Nothing, just getting a bit overheated Coach, I need a water break." Brett inhaled deeply, trying to calm his nerves.

"Yeah, I can see that," Coach answered, blowing his whistle, "water break!"

Just in time thought Brett, admitting to himself that it was really his temper that needed the break. Stepping off to the sideline with a water bottle in hand, he drenched his head and took another deep breath to compose himself.

The entire team raced to gather around Rasheed. Everyone talking at once, they hit Rasheed with a barrage of questions. Geez, everyone is all about him today, Brett thought.

"Hey, Rasheed, where did you get those moves?" Neil the team goalie demanded with a touch of attitude.

Rasheed's dark face was drenched with sweat. He locked eyes with Neil trying to figure out the tone that was coming at him. It had been a trying first day for him, how was he going to ever fit in at this new school. His mother had always advised him to make peace not war.

"My father taught me, he played at Oxford when he was a student there." Rasheed stated calmly with a humble nod.

Listening to the exchange, Brett felt a twinge of resentment. His father had never taught him anything about soccer. Mike Chance had been a two-time, All-

American offensive lineman for Syracuse. The first ball to land in Brett's crib was a football. Brett just never caught on to the game. Soccer was his love.

Coach Bronson tooted the whistle again. Breaking up the chatter, the team gathered around as the coach instructed them to focus on their give and go skills. He divided them for some small-sided games and Brett found himself again defending against Rasheed. Alright, he thought, I'm going to show him I know how to play this game.

But Rasheed was just faster than Brett, he couldn't stop him. His frustration mounted to a frenzy. Rasheed started up the left side of the field handling the ball with precision and finesse. His slim, agile body had the moves of a graceful dancer. Making a smooth, shielded turn he pulled the ball into himself and pirouetted past Brett. Racing to catch up Brett came from behind and hooked Rasheed's right ankle taking him out with a slide tackle.

The force of Coach Bronson's whistle brought the whole team to a dead stop. "Brett that's it, lockers!"

There was a stunned silence, Coach had never thrown anyone out of practice before.

Rasheed got up slowly and offered Brett a hand. Brett ignored Rasheed's gesture of peace. He leaped up, snatched his bag and headed off the field. He didn't even look back as a yell erupted from the team, "Goal! Great corner shot Rasheed!"

Charging across the campus with his head down, he was fuming and oblivious to everything around him. He raced past Ms. Michaels who was leaving for the day. Catching her arm with his bag, her books went flying across the courtyard, papers scattering like leaves blowing in the wind.

Without stopping to help he headed across the parking lot. Hands on hips, she glared at Brett as he raced off. Fingering his key fob, he reached for the car door. Turning, he glanced back at Ms. Michaels and caught her eye as she gathered the papers with the help of several students.

Geez, I can't believe I just did that. She looks really PO'ed he thought. Anger must be contagious. He made a mental note to apologize later.

For the second time today, Brett squealed the Mustang tires as he headed out of the school lot. His books hit the floor as he peeled out of the drive onto Allen's Creek, barely missing a blue "mom taxi" pulling into the school.

It was definitely too early to be home from practice, so Brett took a detour to Geno's. Stepping in the door, he smelled the garlic in the air. The dinner rush was an hour away so Jake, the owner, spotted Brett the minute he opened the door.

"Regular, Brett?" He asked, jotting the order on a small pad.

With a "thumbs up", Brett headed toward a corner table and waited for his Meat Lover's. The mellow lighting and quiet space gave Brett a moment to reflect on the events of the day. His behavior was not who he was. He couldn't figure out where it was coming from. How had he lost control of himself...twice in one day? He was jolted from his thoughts when Jake slid the small, deep dish across the table.

"Pizza can solve all the problems of the world," Jake offered with a creased brow.

It was more a question than a statement. Brett forced a chuckle even though he wasn't feeling it. Although pizza was his favorite, it did little to raise his spirit. Finishing the last bites, he decided enough time had passed and headed for home.

Pulling into the wooded lane on Clover Hills Drive, he sat quietly listening to the last of the Ed Sheeran song playing on his phone. Maddie's favorite! He was trying to think of believable answers for his parent's inevitable questions about his first day back to school. I should just get this over with he thought, heaving a big sigh. He grabbed his books from the floor and his soccer bag from the back seat.

He headed for the side door, hoping he might slip into the two-story house undetected. Brett wasn't looking forward to explaining to his parents that he'd been kicked out of practice. Even though his father didn't know much about soccer, he always insisted that Brett have a strong practice ethic. "You owe it to your team and yourself." He'd heard that more than once while growing up.

Brett's attempted stealth was foiled by Goldie as she pranced back and forth, tangling his legs with each step.

"Brett, is that you?" Can't ever get past mom he thought.

"Yes, Mom," trying to add some enthusiasm to his voice. He failed miserably.

"You want some dinner?" He smelled soup simmering but wasn't interested.

"Not yet, need to clean up first." Brett dodged up the steps to his room.

Pulling his phone from the end of his bag, he glanced at the screen and saw that Maddie had been blowing it up with texts. From the questions she was asking, he could tell the word was out about his practice shenanigans. I can't deal with this now he thought shoving the phone into his pocket.

He tossed his soccer bag in a heap and sauntered across the room. Stacking his books neatly on the corner of his desk, his eyes fell on the picture of Jess and him taken at the annual Paddle and Pour Festival. The family outing was the day before Jessica left for Afghanistan.

They'd browsed through the food and craft booths. Brett had bought Jessica a necklace, a pink quartz stone wrapped in thin, gold wire. She'd been admiring it and he wanted her to have something special from him. Now the necklace was draped across the picture, it had been returned with Jessica's belongings.

Sitting alongside the Erie Canal, savoring sweet berry crepes and waiting for the start of the yearly Regatta, she'd chattered endlessly to Brett about this new page in her life. She was so excited that day, so determined to change the world. Staring at the photo he noticed she'd been fingering the stone necklace. He picked it up and fingered the cold, hard crystal in the same way. He could feel her enthusiasm for her coming adventure radiating from the stone.

He had been so proud of her decision, but now all he felt was anguish. He fell into his bed and pulled the pillow over his head trying to stifle his sobs.

CHAPTER 3

Rasheed arrived at his Aunt Maryam's home after practice worn out and bewildered. Wow, what a day he thought. The aroma wafting through the house told him his aunt had spent the afternoon preparing his favorite, lamb kebobs.

Heading down a narrow hall, Rasheed stopped to look at the framed pictures of his mom and her sister. His mother, Lily, was two years younger but a clone of Aunt Maryam. Rasheed noticed he shared their small, wiry frame and dark eyes. He had the same crooked smile and crowded teeth he saw in the pictures.

He gently caressed his mother's face through the glass. I really need your wisdom today he thought. Totally engrossed in the photos, Aunt Maryam startled him when she gently touched his arm.

"Good afternoon, how did the first day go?" If he closed his eyes the voice could have belonged to his mother.

"It is very kind of you to ask. It was...um, a challenge," he stammered trying to hide his emotions. He didn't want his Aunt thinking he was ungrateful for her gracious hospitality.

"Please, come and eat, we can talk about your day." Her reassuring voice had a calming effect.

Stepping into the modern kitchen, Rasheed saw that dinner was waiting. It was a modest well-kept room, but far surpassed where his family lived in Afghanistan. The scraping of the chair was the only sound in the room as Rasheed settled in front of the waiting meal. They ate quietly. Rasheed began to recoup his energy as the food fueled his tired body.

"Thank you for the wonderful meal, I'm feeling revived." He looked into his Aunt's sweet face.

"Tell me about it." She was very wise to have waited for him to fill up before tackling the topic of his day.

"I'm not sure how to start or if you can understand how different it was from my school back home."

"Remember your mother and I were moved to England in our teen years. We had a similar transition learning about a new school. I will admit we did have one another to rely on when times were difficult. Tell me, what happened today?"

The quiet room was a relief from the bombardment of sounds during his day. The racket of lockers in the school halls, the loud drone in the cafeteria, shouts on the soccer field, so many sounds he had never encountered before. He was grateful it had all been turned off. Now there was only the ticking of the wall clock. Rasheed felt as if he could finally think.

"I suppose things were mostly good. Most people were very nice and very helpful. I just experienced some confrontation from one student, actually twice. He was in my first class and became very upset when I was answering questions about Afghanistan. Then he was at soccer. It was very obvious that he did not like me."

"Curious," she replied nodding her head, encouraging him to continue.

"We played a friendly match at soccer practice, but it didn't seem so friendly for him. I think Brett was his name. He took me down pretty hard." Grimacing as he rolled his shoulders.

"Were you hurt?" There was that sweet concern he often heard from his own mother. Rasheed was more at ease as he continued.

"No, but when I offered a peaceful hand to assist him, his eyes were burning with hate. I have been thinking about this. I don't understand his hate. Why do people behave in this manner?" He asked, picking at the remains on his plate with his fork.

"People have to make a choice as to how they will react in any situation. Tell me, what choice did you make regarding the men who kidnapped you?" Her eyes were studying Rasheed's tired face. Since he had arrived, she had not broached this topic.

"Mother taught me that you will only find peace in your heart if you give peace to others. I guess I have lived with this idea for so long that I would never have considered having hate for those men." Rasheed was pondering his answer, he wasn't deeply religious but he knew hate only bred hate.

"You are very wise for your young years," she replied gently patting his hand. "You need some rest now."

Rasheed rose, placed his dish on the counter and then headed for his small room in the back of the house. He stopped at the door and saw his aunt watching him. "Thank you for listening."

always here." She flashed that crooked

I know why mother sent me here he

sheed ambled across the tidy bedroom and
his books neatly on the corner of a small desk. A
e of his family sat near the desk lamp, he picked it
d studied it closely. It had been taken several days
re he was kidnapped.

His family had gone on an outing to a small park.
uch ventures were always guarded, as terrorist
bombings could erupt without warning. It had been a
peaceful day. He'd never felt closer to his family than
now, staring at their smiles. I miss you all so much he
thought.

Returning the picture to its rightful place, he laid
down on the soft bed. Rasheed fingered the brightly
colored, hand-made throw he was lying on. Scanning
the modest room, he noticed the tribal rug on the
wooden floor and the pictures on the wall of the valley
his family now lived in. His aunt had made every effort
to make him feel at home. It is a privilege to have this
opportunity in America he thought.

Rasheed took a moment to ponder the
conversation with Aunt Maryam. I'm going to make an
effort to understand this Brett's behavior he decided.
Maybe we could be friends. Feeling the need for sleep

he closed his eyes hoping for peaceful dreams. But in his mind's eye he only saw Brett, fuming with hate.

#####

Jessica was surrounded by eager children's faces as she handed out paper and pencils. There was the normal commotion in the makeshift classroom as the students settled into their rough, wooden seats. They were beginning to recite the morning lesson written on an old chalkboard when suddenly noises outside the small hut drowned out their chanting. First there was confusion, then there was stark terror on every face.

An AK-47 was rat-a-ta-tatting through the village. There was screaming and wild pandemonium. The entire class dove for safety. A small child started for the door screaming for his mama. Jessica leaped up sweeping the child into her arms. Then there was blood oozing down her head and a blank expression on her face. Jessica and the child crumpled to the dirt floor. At the door to the school was a young Taliban solider posed with his weapon.

Brett bolted upright, sweat dripping from his brow, his heart racing. He had been having the same dream nightly since they'd received the news of Jessica's death. But tonight, the dream was different. Tonight, the solider was Rasheed!

Brett noticed moonlight was filling his room with the shadows of leaves dancing outside his window. What time is it? How long have I been sleeping? Brett pulled his phone from his pocket where he had last stuffed it, 2 AM. Whew!

Turning on his desk lamp, he opened a drawer and pulled out a pile of letters he had received from Jessica. She'd had no internet access while in Afghanistan, so there had been no emails to update him on her adventures. Brett felt grateful for these few sheets of paper. Somehow, it seemed, he still had a piece of Jess to hold onto. Brett recognized her round, bold handwriting as he opened the last letter he'd received.

Hi Brett,

I can't believe I've been here for almost two months. We are traveling to Shur Abak tomorrow. I'm getting used to traveling around in a Jeep, even though the ride is not as smooth as your 'Stang. ▢ The weather has been dry but hot, in the 90's almost every day. I'm doing OK with the heat but the color brown, UGH! So much sand, it gets into everything! There'll probably be a few pieces falling out of this letter when you open it. LOL!

I'm taking lots of pictures, I can't believe what these people live in, it's a small dome shaped hut made of mud. Can you imagine? I'm amazed how simple their life is. I won't complain ever again, well not much anyway. ☺

I love when we go to a new village, you would think we were some kind of celebrity the way they treat us when we show up. The villagers know we are coming to set up the school. They are really anxious to get their kids out of the fields and into a classroom. Most of the parents are illiterate and they dream of their children having a better life. They know education is the key. Can you imagine that, not knowing how to read or write, wow!

I'm starting to pick up the language. The kids just chatter away when we show up, but I can pick up some of the words and know enough now to say hi and ask their names. We all have different jobs but when we get there we all have to pitch in and unload the supplies to set up the classroom.

It usually takes us about a week to get the school totally up and running. The villages send a couple of their women to Herat to be trained as teachers before we get there. We get the school rolling and then it is over to them to educate their children. Cool, right?

Brett, I can't tell you how happy I am here. I really feel like I am doing something to make a difference. When I see these kid's faces as they learn to read, they are so happy and so thankful. It's worth it for sure!

Tell mom and dad that I'm doing well and I'm very safe. CRS totally monitors the security before we go into any area. I really want to thank you for helping me to convince mom and dad, it's so important what I am doing here. Gotta get some shut eye, we travel early in the AM.

Dooset daram (means Love you!)

Jess

Brett sat up and laid the letter on his desk. Why had she reminded him that he'd convinced their parents that it was safe for her to go? Dropping his head into his hands he remembered the day Jess decided she wanted to go to Afghanistan.

It was late April and spring was in full bloom. The Chance family always attended the 10 AM service at St. Jerome's Church. They always sat in the same pew, third from the front on the left.

Father Bob usually gave a brief, but meaningful sermon. Today he simply introduced Marie Rodriguez, a visitor from Catholic Relief Services. She was speaking about the work she was doing to establish community-based schools in Afghanistan. Brett had been half listening but Jessica was all ears. Ms. Rodriguez was there to solicit funds not volunteers.

After the service Jessica darted straight for the guest speaker and was obviously completely engrossed in their conversation. Brett saw Ms. Rodriguez give Jess a business card and Jess gave her a warm embrace. He had no idea what went on, but he'd never seen his sister beaming like she was that day.

Jessica was quiet all the way home, but to Brett she seemed very content. The next few days she was on the phone nonstop, doing "research" she claimed. Wednesday night, she knocked on Brett's door.

"We need to talk." Brett knew she was conspiring something as she snuck into his room.

"What's up?" He didn't look up from his books.

She didn't hesitate, "I'm going to Afghanistan, but I need your help."

Brett stopped and took a long, serious look at his sister. "Come again?"

"I've been talking to this lady who was at church on Sunday, Ms. Rodriguez. I have all the facts, you know how Dad is. It's all worked out, I can go and help with the schools like she said and I get paid. Did you know that eighty percent of the girls don't get to go to school? I need to help!" She stopped to take a breath.

"Yeah...are you sure? Is it safe? There is a war going on over there you know." Brett wasn't convinced, but could see that Jessica was serious about this. Knowing his sister, once she made up her mind about something it was usually set in stone.

Jess was pacing his room, a pleading expression on her face. He would give into anything when she used this tactic.

"Ms. Rodriguez has been there for eighteen months. She says there is a security team that keeps track of what's happening and she feels safe. She has helped over fourteen thousand kids! She says it is so rewarding. I really feel this is my calling. I'm not sure what I want to study in college, so this is a great way to spend my gap year."

Barely taking a breath, she continued, "Can you imagine all those girls that don't get a chance to have an education? That's just wrong! You have to help me." She seemed to have run down for the moment.

"With what?" Brett had an idea what she was going to say next.

"Convincing Mom and Dad, that's what." She said it like he was crazy to have asked.

So, he did! Please God, forgive me he thought.

Brett looked at his phone, it was 3:10, he needed to sleep. Turning out the light he laid back on his bed. Closing his eyes, he wished for a peaceful sleep, but it didn't come. All he saw was Rasheed with that AK-47 in his hands.

CHAPTER 4

Brett struggled through the week steering clear of Rasheed, both on the field and off. Keeping his attention on soccer and his studies distracted him from thoughts of Jessica. He'd gone a couple of nights without being revisited by his nightmare. That helped! Taking each day as it came, he'd managed to get by, just focusing on the "next thing".

Brett arrived to school early on Friday. Tonight was their season opener, but right now his attention was on Ms. Michaels. Sitting in his car he could see in his mind's eye the expression on her face when he'd run her down Monday. He'd been slinking in and out of class all week avoiding the inevitable.

Today is the day I need to confront this he thought. My apology is long overdue. Brett saw Ms. Michaels pull her silver Prius into the teacher's parking.

"Now's my chance." He grabbed his books and hopped from the car. Racing across the courtyard, he caught up with her at the base of the steps. "Can I help you with your books?" His voice was weak and uncertain.

"Well Brett, that would be nice. To what do I owe this thoughtful gesture?" She stared into his soft blue eyes.

"It's really the least I can do. I need to apologize for my behavior earlier in the week." His gut had that feeling you get when you know you're in for it.

"Brett," she hesitated, "Yes, I was a little upset that day, but I understand you're going through a difficult time. Apology accepted." She unloaded her books into his arms and they headed for her classroom.

Brett breathed a sigh of relief, "Yeah, I don't really understand what was going on with me that day, but I think I'm getting a handle on it."

She stopped and looked him square in the face. "If you need any help, I'm here." Her soft voice defused the tension.

He felt relieved that she hadn't barged into his head any further. Easiest apology ever he thought. You just gotta love Ms. Michaels. He knew she would be there if he asked.

The class was beginning to come alive as they entered the room. Brett delivered her books to the podium up front and Ms. Michaels gave him a polite nod. He skirted the students settling in their seats and headed for the back row. For Brett, there was still comfort in solitude.

Not for long, Maddie hit the door and did a once over of the class. Spotting Brett she headed straight for him.

"Hey, I've been texting all morning." It was more a question than a statement.

"I was busy, I wanted to get here early to handle something." He had completely ignored her text and could see she was annoyed.

"Like what?"

"Just stuff." It was a feeble attempt to appease her and she wasn't buying it.

The bell rang and Maddie plopped down in the desk next to him. Wow, I dodged that bullet he thought, but looking at her he knew it wasn't over. How am I ever going to explain that I've actually been avoiding her.

His thoughts were interrupted when Ms. Michaels pulled out a pile of papers. The class knew they were in for a pop quiz. Time to focus Brett thought.

#####

After class Brett headed straight for the locker room. The players were gathering and there was an electric excitement in the air. Brett's pre-game jitters were compounded by the fact that Coach had invited the Syracuse scouts to the match.

His teammates were hopping around the locker room exchanging light-hearted jokes and encouragement. Brett sat on a bench, eyes closed and head resting against a hard locker, visualizing runs and goals. This was his ritual. He didn't want to change anything.

Above the buzz, he heard someone greet Rasheed. Pictures of the hack he'd landed on him at Monday's practice interrupted his pre-game routine. Shaking his head, Brett tried to shut out the images. He couldn't afford to ruin his focus.

It wasn't long before Coach Bronson called them together. "Alright guys, I know this is our first game so let's just go out there and see what you can put together. Above all else, play for the love of the game.

Let's go!" The team rushed out of the locker room, Brett bringing up the rear.

Trotting onto the field, Brett noticed his coach veer to the sideline and shake hands with two guys in Syracuse jackets. After a brief exchange, Coach Bronson turned and pointed toward Rasheed.

Brett's heart jumped into his throat. Wonder what that's about, he thought. This is supposed to be my chance; my whole future depends on impressing these guys. Everything I've been working toward is coming down to right here, right now! I don't need those guys to be distracted by him.

"Hey, Brett, let's go," a teammate yelled. Brett snapped back to present time and headed toward the open field. Looking over his shoulder he noted where the scouts were settling in the stands.

After the thirty-minute warm-up, Brett had sweat running down his back. He felt loose, he felt good, his ball handling was smooth and effortless. He had purposely stayed away from Rasheed so that he could concentrate on his preparation without distraction.

The ref blew his whistle, calling the team captains to the coin toss. Brett jogged to center field and was surprised to find Rasheed standing next to him waiting. When did this happen, thought Brett, everyone knew he was to be the captain this year. How did this newcomer merit the status? Focus, focus, don't let this guy distract you, Brett nodded to the ref.

"Alright guys, let's have a clean game. Visiting team gets the call." There were quick handshakes all around.

The ref posed for the toss. "Heads," called the Seneca captain as the ref sent the coin flying. Both teams watched it tumble through the air and come to rest in the grass, heads up.

The captains headed for their respective benches. The stands were full and electrified. A wave of blue and white rose from the Wolves' fans as the teams lined up on the field.

A short tweet and play began. Seneca's forward rolled to the right and carried the ball past the first attacker. Out of nowhere, Rasheed stepped in and snatched the ball. Dodging between the black and gold jerseys, Rasheed carried the ball to the top of the penalty box without being challenged. He chipped the ball and sent it sailing over the goalie's hands, it settled in the upper left corner of the net.

The stands erupted as the team raced up to congratulate Rasheed. Brett stood with his hands on his hips eyeing the scouts in the stands. Their heads were together. This can't be good for me he thought.

Trying to shake it off Brett and the Seneca team headed toward center field. Brett's teammates were still celebrating.

Both teams lined up again, Seneca with the ball. Brett noticed the intensity on Rasheed's face. The whistle blew, the Seneca forward drove through the line toward Brett, shielding the ball from Rasheed. Brett assessed the player driving down the line toward him. He read the forward correctly and stepped in for a firm tackle, stealing the ball.

Brett focused on the ball at his feet and tapped it past the halfback, into the open space. Seeing a defender coming on fast he reeled to his right and drove the ball into the corner. A quick glance and he saw Rasheed racing toward the goal. Brett planted his foot and fired the ball toward the center of the box. He watched as Rasheed charged into the space. The goalie snatched the ball out of the air before Rasheed was able to get his head on it.

"Oohhhh!" Erupted the crowd, some relieved, some disappointed. The goalie waited for his team to regroup and booted the ball to mid-field. The Falcon's first attack was stopped short by Allendale's defensive line. The ball was knocked out of bounds after deflecting off of black socks. The blue and white defender picked it up and whipped it over his head down the line toward Brett.

The Falcon's double-teamed Rasheed, so forward movement for the Wolves was being stopped short of the penalty box each time they made an offensive run. The game was like a ping-pong match with the ball bouncing back and forth, neither team finding the reward of the net.

With fifty seconds left in the first half, Allendale got a lucky break. The ball deflected out the end, off a Seneca player, earning the Wolves a corner kick. When the opportunity presented, Coach Bronson called all his players into the penalty box hoping for another score before halftime. Brett settled the ball for the corner kick, he sent it sailing toward its target. With all the blue and white charging, the Seneca defense was overwhelmed and failed to focus on Rasheed. He leaped into the air, perfect timing. His head met the ball before the goalie had a chance to nab it. Score!

The crowd leaped from their seats, there was a deafening roar. The ref blew the whistle signaling half-time. The Wolves, celebrating, headed to the locker room, up 2-0.

"Ok guys, get some water and take a seat." Coach Bronson was moving from player to player complimenting their performance and offering encouragement. When the team had settled from the excitement and hydrated, he outlined the second half strategy. The last few minutes of half-time was counting down as he finished. The team raced to the field, supercharged for the second half.

"Let's huddle up," the coach called his players together, their hands stacked in a pile-up. "One-two-three, go Wolves!" The players let out their traditional howl. The crowd joined in. "OOWWWWWW!"

Trotting onto the field, Rasheed headed toward center half. There was confusion among the Seneca players as they tried to figure out their lineup based on this change.

The ref wasted no time getting the game restarted. The Allendale center forward quickly passed the ball to Brett who ricocheted it past a defender using a sweet give and go. The ball was back at Brett's feet with a wide-open field ahead. But two defenders were zeroing in on him. Brett saw Rasheed coming out of the mid-field, uncontested. The Seneca defenders were scrambling to mark up on all the blue and white headed their way. A smooth pass from Brett put the ball one step ahead of Rasheed. Rasheed did the same pirouette move that had burnt Brett in practice. It was equally effective against the scrambling Falcons. Rasheed got in range and wasted no time taking the shot. Before the ball hit the net, the fans were on their feet.

Brett glared at the scouts in the stands. This whole game was not going as he had envisioned it. I haven't had a chance to show them any of my skills he thought, shaking his head while trotting back to center field. Rasheed is looking like the star with three goals racked up, what if they recruit him and not me?

"Brett!" Coach Bronson yelled from the sidelines. He had a quizzical look on his face. "You alright, son?"

"Sure coach, good." He tried to clear his thoughts, focus!

"OK, get moving," Coach Bronson ordered. Brett looked up and saw that the rest of the team was waiting on him.

As play continued the Wolves were clearly in control. The black and gold players failed to get any offense ignited and spent the next fifteen minutes scrambling to keep the ball out of the net. Despite the ongoing attack, the Seneca goalie made several brilliant saves and the score remained 3-0.

With ten minutes left in the game, a Wolves defender stole a ball from a Seneca player mounting a strong attack. The defensive line put together a good combination of passes bringing the ball out of the back and hit Rasheed center field. Rasheed saw Brett open on the right and sent a brilliant pass his way through two defenders. Brett charged the ball and gaining full possession, he carried it up the line. He stalled for a brief moment to assess the position of his teammates.

I don't want to give this ball to Rasheed again he thought, but there were no other players open. Watching Brett, the goalie moved to the right side of the box anticipating a shot. Brett made a snap decision and sent the ball to the open space at the top of the goal box. Rasheed had read him like a book and was in the space as the ball arrived. With pure finesse, he softly tapped the ball into the left corner catching the goalie flat footed.

It was 4-0, Rasheed is a one-man team thought Brett watching his teammates rally around him.

"Rasheed," Coach Bronson signaled him off the field and replaced him with a sophomore who had been showing promise in practice.

"Brett, center half." Coach instructed. Alright, my turn thought Brett. He was goal hungry. He glanced into the stands and saw the scouts heading out of the stadium. His heart fell to the pit of his stomach. His opportunity to impress them was over before it had started.

The last minutes of the game were uneventful with neither team able to get the ball within range of the goal. The ref tweeted his whistle signaling the end of the game. The fans flew out of the stands heading across the field.

It was a sweet victory and the team celebrated by dumping the remaining ice water on Rasheed. He was now fully initiated into the group! Brett didn't join in on the celebrating. He had no desire to be reminded that Rasheed was the star of the game.

He trudged to the locker behind the rest of the team. Coach Bronson congratulated individual players on notable plays, but Brett wasn't listening. Things had not turned out in his favor.

Coach Bronson turned them loose for the night after brief instructions for practice times next week. The rest of the team boisterously left the locker. Brett gathered his things and dodged around the celebrating, heading for his car.

Madison caught up with him as he opened the car door.

"Brett, everyone's going to Geno's, you coming?" She threw her arms around his neck. "That was an awesome game!"

"Yeah, some game." Not for me he thought.

"What's up? Come on, let's get some pizza?"

"Naw, I have homework." He dodged into his car ignoring her invitation. Revving the engine, he backed out and took off leaving Madison in a complete mystery.

CHAPTER 5

On Monday morning, the students at Allendale were still celebrating Friday night's decisive win. Rasheed was in the spot light. Brett watched as back slaps and high fives were offered by students who hadn't ever spoken to him. Looks like there is a new celebrity in town he thought.

The mood was subdued as he entered American Government. The room was dark with a video posed to begin, faces from across the globe populated the screen. As the students entered the room a kind of reverence overtook them. When the bell finished its last chime, Ms. Michaels started the video. Pictures of strife and violence followed, with harrowing facts being spewed by the narrator.

"There are 195 nations on earth. In 55 there is no right to a fair trial, in 128 countries freedom of expression is restricted and in 141 people are tortured."

The screen froze, lights came on and there was complete silence in the room. Brett was stunned by some of the horrific pictures he had seen.

"What are human rights?" Ms. Michaels posed staring hard into the reserved expressions of her students. No one offered an immediate response; the silence was as thick as a fog.

A hand rose timidly in the back. "Yes?" Ms. Michaels encouraged the brave volunteer.

"Well, from what we saw, I guess a fair trial and freedom of speech are human rights."

"Great, any other ideas?" Ms. Michaels was aiming to stretch her student's imaginations.

"Well, is it just rights we have because we are human?" offered Zoe from the front row.

"That's a fair generalization." Ms. Michaels was hunting for more; the students were used to her tactics.

Kaden, the class clown chimed in, "Is there some list somewhere?" The smile on Ms. Michaels face proved he was getting hot.

"As a matter of fact, there is." Ms. Michaels lowered the lights again and "The Story of Human Rights" began. Following a timeline through history, the concept of human rights was outlined starting with Cyrus the Great in Babylon and ending with the formation of the "Universal Declaration of Human Rights" created by the United Nations.

"Well, where is this list then?" Kaden wanted answers.

Ms. Michaels began distributing small booklets that outlined the document created by the United Nations. Chatter and page shuffling broke the silence. Students were quietly discussing among themselves particular points of interest as Ms. Michaels finished handing out the materials. Brett remained silent flipping through the pages.

"Okay class, as you see there are 30 points on this document and as the video described the declaration was agreed upon by all nations of the UN following the end of World War II." Ms. Michaels directed the attention of the students. "We are going to spend some time going through each of these points and discussing their application in your life."

"I see why we are doing this now, after studying the holocaust, but that was then. I don't see how it has application in our lives today." Lucas was being his normal confrontationist.

Ms. Michaels hesitated, "OK." She gave the class a minute to ponder the comment.

"I do," mumbled Brett.

"In what way?" The ball was rolling. Ms. Michaels wanted to keep Brett talking, this was the first time he had offered an opinion in class since his sister's death.

"Well, the video said people have a right to life. I think that means no one else has the right to take another's life." Brett clammed up, he had already said more than he wanted.

"Great point." Noticing the distress on Brett's face, Ms. Michaels offered him a way out. "Let's watch this short clip and then we'll continue with that point." Lights out and a brief description of article three played, the Right to Life.

When the lights went up Ms. Michaels recited some brief facts, "An estimated 6,500 people were killed in 2007 in armed conflict in Afghanistan—nearly half being noncombatant civilian deaths at the hands of insurgents. Hundreds of civilians were also killed in suicide attacks by armed groups."

Add my sister to that list thought Brett. Fortunately, Ms. Michaels turned her attention to Rasheed.

"I wanted to bring up this point because I thought Rasheed could give us some firsthand information about what is happening in his country." Brett relaxed now that the attention was diverted.

"Yes, there are many tragedies in my country," Rasheed hesitated.

"Tell us what's going on there." Zoe's voice offered compassion and she seemed truly interested, so Rasheed continued.

"Well, there are many factions fighting over the rights to the poppy fields. In the Helmand Valley, where my family lives, half of the farmland is planted with the poppy plant."

"Well, why don't they plant something else?" Lucas offered what seemed to be a logical solution.

Rasheed continued his explanation, "The farmers are very poor and they are threatened with death if they do not comply and plant poppies. They have no choice, they are just trying to provide for their family. There is not much they can do if they want to live and protect their loved ones."

"Wow!" Several girls voiced in unison. There were tears in their eyes, this was a new concept to them.

"How can this be allowed?" asked Zoe. Rasheed shrugged, not having a logical answer.

"There is another point I would like to take up," Ms. Michaels interrupted. "Let's watch this clip." The article, No Slavery, played briefly.

"Ms. Michaels, slavery was outlawed a long time ago, right?" The students were trying to digest the uncomfortable information.

"Well yes, as the video explained, but listen to this fact: The US State Department estimates 600,000 to 820,000 men, women and children are trafficked across international borders each year, half of whom are minors."

Ryan, sitting in the back jumped in, "I was watching a documentary that said human trafficking is at an all-time high in the US. It said there are more people being held against their will now then during the 1800s when slavery was legal."

"That's true, it's a huge problem in the US. There are probably people right in our own community who are being held as slaves." Ms. Michaels could tell by her student's expressions that she was getting through to them.

"I have one more video then we can discuss these few points more in depth." She played article five, No Torture or Cruel, Inhuman Degrading Treatment. There was silence in the class as the lights came back on.

"I was hoping Rasheed would help us out here again. Anything else you can add about your country regarding this point?" She looked straight at him but saw that Rasheed had gone pale. He looked to be in a state of shock. Something had happened. She didn't push the point.

Shifting her attention to the entire class, she continued, "I want to share another fact with you: In 2008, US authorities continued to hold 270 prisoners in Guantánamo Bay, Cuba, without charge or trial, subjecting them to "water-boarding," torture that simulates drowning. As you see, there are human rights violations right in our own backyard, so to speak."

"I have your assignment for tonight," she added.

"Awww," a unanimous agreement went up from the class.

"I chose these three points first because they are somewhat related. I want you to do some internet research and find current incidents of these three violations. I'll give you an example from the American past. The African Americans were held as slaves and many times tortured if they did not work hard enough. Repeat offenders were often killed as an example to other slaves to behave accordingly. See if you can find incidents of these three rights being violated today."

"Does it have to be just in America?" The question came from the back of the room.

"Not necessarily, see what you can find. Come prepared tomorrow." The bell rang as Ms. Michaels wrapped up.

Brett sat quietly thinking over the assignment. Then he noticed Rasheed, his head down on his desk, he looked in complete despair. Wonder what's up with him, thought Brett.

Ms. Michaels slid over to Rasheed and gently placed her hand on his shoulder. Rasheed's head popped up and Brett could see that he had tears in his eyes.

"What's going on Rasheed?" Ms. Michaels voice was full of compassion.

"Well, I don't want to be rude, but I cannot discuss this right now. I must go home." Rasheed leaped from his chair and darted out the door. Ms. Michaels looked bewildered.

Brett offered to help, "Do you want me to chase him down?"

"No, I'll handle him later, you should get to your next class." Ms. Michaels, standing at her door, watched Rasheed's retreat toward the exit.

#####

The lunchroom ruckus was at a normal pitch, with teachers mingling among the tables diverting any potential incidents. Brett entered the room and did a brief once over, they are all so oblivious, he thought. The videos from American government were still fresh in his memory. Making a beeline to his normal table, he sat down to a conversation already in progress.

"Hey Brett," the greeting was brief as they continued the discussion.

"I was really shocked," Brett saw the concern on Madison's face as she spoke. He knew from experience that she was in "serious" mode.

"What's the story," he asked, trying to edge into the dialogue.

"We were talking about Ms. Michael's class assignment," Kaden brought him up to speed.

"Yeah, I just can't imagine how people can be so cruel to others," Madison's brow was strained. "I didn't know people were still kept as slaves today. It's just so unreal in my world."

"I think that's what Ms. Michaels was getting at, she wants us to look outside our safe, little bubble," Brett's serious tone received nods of agreement around the table.

"I was on the internet during study hall and found out that kids our age in some countries are taken as soldiers, they give them drugs and make them do horrible things." Zoe was trembling, Brett felt her pain.

"What about that stuff Rasheed said about people being kil..." Lucas froze midsentence. It was too late to swallow his words. "Sorry Brett." He offered a feeble apology.

The air among the group was electric; silence hung for several minutes. Brett knew all eyes were on him, his heartbeat pounded like a bass drum in his head.

"You're a jerk," Kaden punched Lucas in the arm breaking the spell. A solid agreement was offered up by everyone at the table. Lucas was out of line.

"It's OK," Brett tried to ease the tension.

"Hey, where's Rasheed?" Madison shifted the conversation. No one had seen him since first period.

"Well, he was definitely upset after class." Brett explained what he had witnessed and how Rasheed had raced out of school.

"I hope he's OK, maybe he has some kind of bad memories, I mean does anyone know why he's here without his family?" Curiosity was one of Madison's obsessive traits.

"I'm pretty sure something was going on with him," Brett added, "but we all have bad memories we have to learn to live with."

Before Madison could reply the bell rang. The cafeteria emptied in a flash with students bumping off each other like pinballs, heading to fourth period.

#####

After class Brett made his way to the practice field and joined his teammates in stretching warm-ups. The players were chattering among themselves, still reliving the highlights of the game and the new star player. Brett ignored the conversation.

"Alright guys, let's get started." Coach Bronson called them together. "First, great game Friday! Today, we are going to focus on a few points I noticed in the game films."

Hmmmm...no Rasheed, Brett noticed at the same time the coach did.

"Where's Rasheed?" Coach Bronson inquired. The team members shrugged in unison. No one seemed to have an answer.

Of course, he's worried about his new star, thought Brett. But this could be an opportunity for me. Brett cleared his mind and focused on the coach's words.

"First thing we are going to work on is the quality of your first touch, maintaining control of the ball and getting off the pass to the open man. You need to maintain possession by protecting the ball then look for the clean open pass."

As Coach explained the drill, Brett concentrated on how to keep his touch soft and directed so that he could set up the perfect pass. With his efforts focused, Brett felt in full control of the ball. Now this is more like it, he thought, I'm the force on the field.

It was a cool, crisp afternoon but after about forty-five minutes of running the drill, the team was in need of a water break. While they were mulling around the water station, Coach Bronson switched the focus of the practice to their finishes.

"In the offensive attack, we need to make smart runs but I want you to feel comfortable enough to take a risk. Trust yourself to beat the defensive player one on one. If you are double teamed, look for the open man but be ready to rush the net. If the goalie misses the ball or a defender has a bad touch you should be ready for the easy score. Ok. This is the drill."

As Coach Bronson explained the drill they were about to run, Brett could easily visualize himself making the runs and the easy tap into the net. Not a fancy shot, but still a score. Counts all the same, he thought.

Brett felt his confidence build as he placed shot after shot in the corner of the net. He was in good spirits when the coach called an end to the practice.

"Hey, Brett." Coach Bronson called to him as they were picking up the balls and cones scattered around the field.

"Yeah?" Brett trotted over, still glowing from what he felt was a successful practice. "I felt great today, more like my old self. What did you think?"

"I want to go over a few things with you. My plans for the year and helping you with your goals." Coach wanted all of Brett's attention.

"Well, we've talked about a scholarship, I know with everything going on with Jess..." he stopped and composed himself. "I still have that as my goal." Brett gained control of his trembling voice.

"I'm sure you do, but with Rasheed showing up, I've changed my game strategy a bit."

Brett was stunned, he wasn't quite sure where this was going.

"I noticed that your attention was stuck on those scouts at the game, you seemed rattled. You have to keep your attention on the field."

"OK," Brett answered hesitantly.

"You're not the only star on the field now."

Brett felt stung by those words, he had always been the star and wasn't sure he wanted to share the limelight.

Coach Bronson continued, trying not to lose Brett's attention, "You both have different talents and skills, I think if the two of you work together it will bring our team to a whole new level."

"We don't know how long Rasheed will be here, it's not like he'll be around for a scholarship. I really want to be sure that the scouts see what I can do." Brett was thinking about Maddie's words at lunch. What is Rasheed doing here, he thought?

"I promise you that the scouts will see your strengths. Remember they are looking for a rounded player, one that can use his teammates to make key plays. Not a one-man team."

Brett thought back to the plays he had made with Rasheed that ended with the ball in the net. He was used to being the scorer, but he did have the assist.

"I want the scouts to see that I can score," Brett felt stuck on the fact that Rasheed had scored all of the points in the game.

"What did we just focus on in practice?" Coach Bronson wanted Brett to come to the realization on his own. He saw when the light went on!

"Listen Brett, I'll do everything to help you reach your goals. I won't jeopardize your chance at a scholarship, but you have to trust me and work with me. Rasheed is an asset for you and for our team. I want you to have the best season you can have, alright?"

"Ok, Coach," Brett's shell was cracking, "but don't expect me to be his friend. Who knows, he could leave back to Afghanistan tomorrow."

"Yes, he could. But for now, just give me a chance. I'd never compromise your hopes for the future. Besides, you know I rely on you to keep the team pumped and focused while on the field. That's definitely one of your strengths. Let's have a fun season, alright?" Coach Bronson wanted Brett's agreement.

"Alright." Brett didn't have any reason not to trust his coach.

"Great! You should get out of here now, see you tomorrow." The seriousness of the conversation was gone.

Brett gathered his things, heading toward his Mustang. Dusk was settling as Brett pulled his car out of the school lot, heading for home. So many things have changed, this year is not going as I expected he thought.

His grandpa's face popped into his mind's eye. Change had always been hard for him as a kid. He recalled when he was in kindergarten, Brett was upset because his mom took a new job and wasn't going to be able to drop him at school in the morning. He was sitting at breakfast crying and Gramps was listening to him go on about all the reasons why she had to take him to school.

When he was finally cried out, Gramps had imparted one of his "pearls". "You know Brett, life is about change. If we don't change then we get stuck in time and never grow. Can you imagine being in your five-year-old body forever?"

Brett remembered the picture he had gotten of himself going off to work in a shirt and tie with a briefcase, as a five-year-old. It had gotten him and Gramps laughing so hard that he almost peed his pants.

The memory eased Brett's tension over the conversation with Coach. Gosh Gramps, you're still looking out for me he thought. I miss you!

He pulled into the drive at home feeling that maybe he could make the changes his coach wanted. He grabbed his gym bag and jumped out of the car, headed for the door. I wonder what's for dinner, I'm starved!

CHAPTER 6

Rasheed peddling his bike was headed for home. Out of nowhere he is blinded by a black hood thrown over his head. Thrashing his arm and legs, he tries to beat off the offender. Then he feels a sharp prick in his arm and loses consciousness.

When he wakes his tongue is as dry as the Rigestan desert. The cold, dark room is barely large enough for him to stretch his full length. The hard, sand floor has left him cramped and dirty.

"Where am I?" He struggles to pull himself out of the fog hanging over from the drug cocktail.

"Hello," he yells hoping someone would come to his rescue but he knows that won't be the case.

"Ah, the little prince has awakened," the voice behind the door is harsh and mocking.

Rasheed didn't want to imagine what was going to happen next. He knew that it was common for young boys to be kidnapped and used for savage purposes.

"This can't be good," he mutters still struggling to clear his head. Where am I he wonders. How many times has father warned me? What nightmare is this?

The lock rattles and he is faced with his captor.

"Come prince, Mullah wants to see the prize we have brought him." The evil in his voice ran cold chills down Rasheed's spine.

"Why do you call me prince?" Rasheed speaks boldly, hoping to cover his fear.

"You think you are so special because your father is an important man. You will see how special you are to Mullah."

Rasheed tries to place that name as he is dragged along a dark, damp hall and into an open room. Then he is face to face with Mullah Sharif Anis. Panic strikes!

He flashes back to the day this man stopped his father on the street demanding payment to pass. Rasheed had been so proud of his father standing up to this vile creature. But now he is face to face with the devil. He doesn't possess the courage of his father.

Rasheed woke with someone gently shaking his shoulder. He pulled himself out of the abyss and was relieved to be staring into the soft face of Aunt Maryam. Drenched in sweat, shaking violently, he clutched his aunt's hand. His lifeline to reality.

She switched on the desk lamp. Scanning the soft shadows in the room, Rasheed inhaled deeply.

"You were screaming in your sleep, but you are safe my son." Rasheed broke into tears.

"I am here. You are safe," she repeated in her serene manner.

"I have not had that dream since I arrived here, I hoped I had left it in Afghanistan." Sitting up in his bed, Rasheed wrapped his arms around his shoulders attempting to control the tremors racking his body.

"Your mother was wise to send you here. But you cannot escape the demons you buried in your mind. Being in a new place has put them to sleep, but a smell, a sound, a touch, anything can bring back to you the nightmare you lived." She paused studying Rasheed's face. "Tell me what happened today." Aunt Maryam's soothing tone brought calm to his jagged nerves.

"We had a discussion in class this morning about Human Rights. Ms. Michaels wanted me to share my knowledge of the kinds of torture that occurs in Afghanistan. She was not being cruel. She did not know.

But I'm afraid she was the one who woke the sleeping demons." Tears streamed down Rasheed's caramel colored cheeks.

"I see. I felt something was wrong when you came home." Aunt Maryam handed Rasheed a tissue. Softly rubbing his shoulder, she waited for him to continue.

"There is more I have to tell you," Rasheed hesitated, gathering his thoughts. "I could not stay at school so I went to a park with my soccer ball. I'm sorry I didn't tell you I left school, but I couldn't talk about it."

"Rasheed, no man can ever hide from his nightmares. One must have the courage to confront his demons or they will forever chase you and rule your life."

"I appreciate your wisdom Aunt Maryam, but I'm afraid I will never be able to confront my tormentors." The nightmare was still fresh in his mind.

"Rasheed, you are safe here, whatever happened is now in the past with only the memories remaining." She stopped, looking deep into Rasheed's eyes, "But may I ask, what can a memory do to you?" She waited for him to fully absorb the question.

Rasheed took a deep breath, he was far away now, back in that dungeon in Afghanistan.

"Have you heard of Mullah Sharif Anis?" He paused to see his aunt's reaction.

"I have heard of the evil ways of this man, he is a small-time crook who hooked up with the Taliban. He does not fight for a cause, he fights only for money. But I have also heard that he finds sick joy in taking young boys for his perverted pleasure." Aunt Maryam studied Rasheed's face. "Did this happen to you?"

Rasheed hid his face as his tears flowed freely. Aunt Maryam held him close while he quietly sobbed. He had not shared his story with anyone but somehow this sweet lady had unraveled the truth.

After what seemed an eternity, Rasheed ran out of tears. "I am so ashamed," he whispered.

"What did you do to be ashamed of?" Her sweet voice encouraged Rasheed to continue.

He looked into his aunt's soft, brown eyes, "I wasn't brave like my father, I did not stand up to this man and stop him."

"I see," was all she said.

But those two words eased Rasheed's guilt. There was no shame or blame in her tone, there was only understanding. Rasheed felt a bond growing.

"Thank you," he hugged her until he feared he might crack her fragile bones.

"You must sleep now, you have school." She rose and headed for the door.

"Aunt Maryam, please don't tell anyone," he pleaded.

"I don't have to, you will when you are ready." She turned out the lights and gently closed the door.

Rasheed stared at the shadows on the ceiling, rewinding their conversation. She is right, he thought. Demons can only haunt you if you are not willing to confront them. He closed his eyes and slept a peaceful rest.

#####

Brett arrived late to school the next morning and headed straight for the administration office. He was happy to see that the small space was buzzing with students coming and going. As a result, no one questioned his tardiness. On the sign in sheet he wrote that he had overslept, but deep down he knew he didn't want to be part of the discussion in American Government. His research homework had resulted in another nightmare. I'll talk to Ms. Michaels later, he thought, heading for second period.

Brett kept to himself as the day slipped by, his thoughts were on yesterday's conversation with Coach Bronson. He had talked to his dad after practice to get his input on the coach's strategy. Being a football player, Michael Chance didn't know much about soccer but believed in strict discipline where any sports training was concerned. He had basically told Brett that his coach's decisions were not to be questioned and that's what would be expected of him in college, so get used to it! The conversation went pretty much how Brett predicted. Falling asleep, he had decided he needed to trust his coach to help him reach his goal.

Now, sitting in sixth period he was oblivious to the teacher's words. He was deep in thought. All the frustration of the first game replayed in his mind in slow motion. Between a future scholarship and nightmares about Jessica it seems my mind never shuts off. When did life get so complicated he wondered.

The bell snapped him out of his trance. Gathering his books and heading for his locker, he realized the only place he found true peace was on the field with the ball at his feet. Playing the game, pushing his body and focusing on putting the ball in the goal, somehow cleared his mind.

As he grabbed his book bag from the open locker, his phone went off. Pulling it from the side pouch he saw Maddie's sweet smile light up the screen. He let it roll to voice mail. I need to get to practice he thought.

Within seconds, a text popped up. "Meet me at the stable after soccer. Luv, Maddie."

Standing posed with the phone in his hand, a slew of answers raced through his mind. He envisioned a multitude of scenarios to every possible response. Don't have time for this, he thought. Reluctantly he typed, "Sure."

Approaching the field, Brett saw that Coach Bronson had pulled Rasheed aside. He kept an eye on them during warm-ups. He noticed that Coach Bronson, hands on Rasheed's shoulders, had an intense expression on his face. I wonder what that's about he thought. He hadn't seen Rasheed all day, but seeing them now locked in this all-consuming conversation, Brett wondered if Rasheed was OK. He actually felt concerned about him as a person—where did that come from?

Wrapping up the warm-ups, Coach Bronson got the team started on a rerun of the drills from the day before. Brett walked over to Rasheed and tossed the ball to his feet.

"Come on, one-on-one. I'll show you what we worked on yesterday."

The surprised expression on Rasheed's face told all. "Alright!"

Soon they were both engrossed in the world of soccer, trying to best each other, but encouraging one another after any goal scored. Coach Bronson was pleased.

#####

The parking lot at Lehman Stables was virtually empty as Brett swung the 'Stang into a space usually reserved for boarders. He sat for a moment trying to gather some courage, he had a premonition that this conversation wasn't going to go well.

Gathering his wits, he stepped from the car and headed into the stable. Bruno came running to greet him, tongue hanging wildly to the side aiming to plant a sloppy kiss on his friend.

"Hey, Bruno, I see by your excitement meter that I'm top on your list tonight, you could beat someone up with that tail." Brett stooped and ruffled the dog's fur. Well, someone is happy to see me he thought.

"Come on, let's find Maddie," Brett headed down the empty aisle, Bruno dancing in circles around him. Outside Midnight's stall was a wheel barrel piled high with mulch, manure and topped with a pitchfork. Peeking around the corner he saw Madison, hoof pick in hand, flipping dirt clods from a soft sole.

"Hey!" Brett reached up and gently caressed Midnight's Muzzle.

"Oh, hey, I wasn't sure you would come," Madison glanced briefly at Brett and went back to the work at hand.

"I said I would." Brett stopped, he didn't want a confrontation.

"I have been getting the feeling you were avoiding me." He could see that she was a bit fired up.

"Been busy with school and soccer, trying to work things out." He reached over to her tack box and grabbed a carrot that Midnight was eyeing.

"But I didn't see you all day, what happened?" Madison was as intent on his answer as she was on the hoof she was working over.

"Well, I overslept this morning…"

Before he could finish Maddie interrupted, "I thought maybe you were just skipping that American Government discussion."

"I don't know, maybe." She knows me too well he thought.

"Then you weren't at lunch, where were you?" She asked, running the third degree on him.

"I had to go see Ms. Michaels," Brett made a mental note to remember that little white lie. "What gives Maddie? I just came to visit."

Shaking her head and murmuring under her breath, Maddie dropped Midnight's hoof and looked straight into his blue eyes.

"Okay." Bewilderment was written all over her face. "I'm sorry, it's just that I've been missing you and I've been feeling like you didn't want to talk to me." After voicing what had been pent up inside, her face softened. She moved to the next hoof and waited for Brett to offer an explanation.

"I'll be honest," he began slowly, "every time we are together you want to talk about Jessica. I just can't do it."

"Well, I'm just trying to help. I thought talking would help you to deal with it." She paused waiting for a response. "You know, maybe you're not the only one having a tough time."

"I'm working on it in my own way!" His terse comment was an effort to put an end to the subject, but this was the first time he even considered that maybe Maddie needed to talk about Jess's death.

Maddie got it. Hoping to salvage the visit she quickly changed the topic "How was practice?"

Brett felt his insides calm. "It was great, Rasheed and I were working on some drills together. I think Coach Bronson was happy with our progress."

"I really like Rasheed. But, you know he refused to talk today in government. It was weird, he basically told Ms. Michaels that he couldn't participate. She didn't push it. But it was strange, the whole class was stunned that he talked to her like that. I think maybe something horrible happened to him."

Madison was always analyzing people's behavior and more often than not she was dead on. It was like she had a magic portal into people's thoughts.

So what, he thought, horrible things happen to lots of people.

"I don't want to talk about Rasheed!" Brett barked.

"Jeez Brett, you brought him up." The conversation was draining Maddie's patience.

"Ok! Ok, I'm sorry." Seeing Maddie was done with Midnight's hooves and knowing her routine, he handed her the dandy brush.

"When is your next show?" He was desperately trying to find a topic that wouldn't get either of them peeved.

That was it, when Maddie talked horses the rest of the world waited. Watching her face light up as she described her goals for the next event, Brett realized that horses were as much her sanctuary as the soccer field was his.

She talked until she finished brushing Midnight, then Brett helped her pack up the tack box and lock up the stall. Strolling down the aisle, headed for their cars,

Maddie grabbed Brett's arm and pulled him to an abrupt stop.

"I'll see you tomorrow?" It was definitely a question not a statement.

He stared into her beautiful blue eyes, then placed a tender peck on her check.

"Sure," he whispered softly. Reaching his car, he turned and saw she was still watching him. He blew her a kiss.

Pulling out of the lot, a text popped up, "Luv you, Maddie!" Relief washed over his body as he headed for home. We'll get past this, he thought, as soon as I can un-complicate my world!

CHAPTER 7

Entering American Government the next morning, Brett saw Ms. Michaels was already busy preparing for the day's lesson. She eyed him as he headed for the back row. Before he could settle in his seat she was behind him.

"I'm not trying to make you uncomfortable in class Brett, if today's discussion is too much for you feel free to take a break." Brett figured she had already guessed why he didn't show up yesterday.

Wow, a teacher giving me an excuse to skip class thought Brett. Leave? Stay? Leave?

Stay? Before he could make up his mind, Maddie showed up at the door scanning the room. Zeroing in on Brett, she headed his way.

Brett took a deep breath, I wonder which direction this is going to go he thought.

"Good morning Brett, thanks for visiting me last night." She plopped into the chair beside him flashing her sweet smile.

There was no decision to be made now, how could he possibly explain to her what he was doing if he packed up his books and left? Sliding into his seat, he reached over and grabbed her hand.

"I'm excited for you and your upcoming horse show." It was a safe topic for discussion. Before she could reply the bell rang and the jumble of students settled into their desks.

"It was a great discussion yesterday. We are going to explore a few other human rights articles today, so take out your 'Story of Human Rights' booklets." Ms. Michaels didn't mess around when she was excited about a topic.

"How many of you would say you have ever experienced a tough living condition?" It was an unusual question but of course Kaden had a quick response.

"I went camping once, that was tough, you know, no toilets." He got the reaction he was fishing for as a chuckle rippled through the class. Gradually, hands shot up.

"I remember when our house had a fire, we had to live in a trailer for a while when it was being repaired. That was pretty rough, especially since I got the couch all the time." Everyone had heard Chloe's story before, so no one was surprised.

"Noah," Ms. Michaels was interested to see his hand, as he seldom participated in the class discussions.

"Well, I don't think anyone knows, but I'm adopted." The class turned in unison, all eyes on him. "My real mom was a drug addict. When I was really little I was taken from her. All I remember is sitting by her, hungry and crying but she wouldn't wake up. That was tough." The class was stunned, several of the girls wiped a tear from their eyes.

"Thank you for sharing that Noah. That was a tough situation," Ms. Michaels' compassion showed she was as surprised as the rest of the class.

Wow, you really never know what people are living with thought Brett. He glanced at Madison as she crumpled a tissue in her hand. Noah was the quiet kid in the class. They had all just been given a window into his life they'd never suspected.

"Let's look at the two clips that relate to the articles we are going to study today, then we will open the floor for discussion." Lights went out and "Human Right 26, Food and Shelter for All" came up on the TV screen followed by the "Right to Education". When they finished playing, the class was silent.

"Take a moment and read articles 25 and 26 in your booklets," Ms. Michaels wanted to make an impact.

Reading about the right to education transplanted Brett back to his conversation with Jessica. He could still hear her passion. She was so distraught that girls in Afghanistan didn't receive an education.

Ms. Michaels jolted him from his recall. "Here are some interesting statistics, three billion people make less than $2.50 a day and over 80% of the world's population lives on less than $10 a day."

Kaden popped up, "I spend more than that at Starbucks!"

"That's not funny!" Zoe couldn't hold her tongue. "Those people live in a world I can't even imagine. I have everything I need, I get to go to this nice school, I have all the food I need..."

"Yeah, we all know, you're the best dressed in school." Kaden laughed at his dig.

"Ok, let's not do that Kaden, Zoe is getting my point. We live a comfortable life here in the US." Ms. Michaels took control of the discussion. "I want to share two videos, the first is titled 'Kids at work, out of school in Afghanistan' and the other is 'Girls struggle for an Education.' Watch them with the two articles you just read in mind."

The first clip was a stark representation of life in Afghanistan. The class watched, spell bound, as they witnessed kids their own age working long hours each day sitting at a weaver's loom. Some may go to school but most were required to work all day to help support their family. Other kids were employed as metal workers sometimes suffering injuries from the metals they cut. There were kids working as bonded laborers making bricks to pay off a family debt, some as young as five. It was a reality they weren't prepared for and the shock on their faces testified to the tragedy of the situation.

Ms. Michaels had them on the edge of their seats, so she didn't waste any time queuing up the second video. A dusty, brown landscape was the backdrop to the torn tents that the young Afghan girls called school. Packed like sardines, sitting on a hard dirt floor they recited their lessons while Afghan boys sat comfortably in a classroom still rough by American standards, but a much-improved situation compared to what qualified for school for the girls. Some of the students walked over an hour to get to school. Then there was always the threat of acid attacks and kidnappings, so many girls just stopped going to school.

The video showed Brett the bleak truth of the world Jessica had experienced. This kind of tragedy had always tugged at Jess's heart strings. She could never let an injustice go unchecked. That's just the kind of person she was.

When the lights came up the whole class was staring at Rasheed.

"Was that the kind of school you went to before you came here?" Heads were nodding in unison before Emma even finished the query. There was a renewed curiosity regarding Rasheed's life in Afghanistan.

Taking a deep breath Rasheed tried to paint a picture of his life before Allendale. "No, I did not go to one of those schools. I think I explained, my mother and father were educated in England. When my father got his job at the dam and we moved to Afghanistan, my mother taught my sister and I at home."

"Wait," Kaden, always the loud mouth, "you never told us you have a sister, is she still there?"

"How old is she?"

"Why isn't she here?" Questions were flying.

"Hold on," Ms. Michaels wanted to get the discussion under control. "Rasheed if you are comfortable telling us about it, we would love to hear about your life there.

"My sister is ten, my mother still teaches her every day. She is too young to be away from home." Rasheed began to squirm.

"You never told us why you were here." That was the question Rasheed didn't want to answer. Ms. Michaels noticed his fidgeting and rapidly changed the direction of the conversation.

"Brett, do you have any insight about Afghan schools."

Brett took a deep breath, trying to muster his courage. My sister was brave enough to venture into such a world, he thought, I should honor her spirit. He gave a brief nod so Ms. Michaels forged ahead.

"Do you know what kind of schools Jess worked in?"

"She worked for one of those CBE organizations they talked about, they went to villages and helped them set up schools. I know she loved what she was doing." His voice faltered.

Brett had captured Rasheed's attention, his gaze locked on Brett, "Your sister was in Afghanistan?" He sounded horrified, "My country is a very dangerous place for girls," he seemed to rethink his statement, "No, my country is very dangerous for anyone."

"I know." Brett had said all he could, "Can I be excused Ms. Michaels?"

"Sure Brett." The class was shocked that she'd given in so easily.

As the door closed behind him, Brett heard the discussion continue.

"Ms. Michaels, what's an acid attack?" He didn't stick around to find out.

Brett stepped into the cafeteria and did a once over of the lunchtime ruckus. Heading toward his normal table he stopped short when he saw Rasheed sitting with his friends. All attention was on Rasheed. I wonder what that's about he thought. Not wanting to find out, he did a quick about face and headed outdoors toward the school's nature trail. It didn't measure up to the trails at Corbett's Glen but it gave him some time to be alone and think things out.

He headed down the trail winding his way toward the tennis courts. The sky was overcast and most of the trees were naked of their leaves. The dismal gray matched his mood. Fortunately, the path was empty. His thoughts were on his sister. The videos in American Government had given him food for thought. He was only beginning to understand the things that Jess had seen and done in Afghanistan. It felt weird, it was the first time in their lives that he didn't know everything about her. His heart ached.

His thoughts were interrupted by the vibration of the phone in his pocket. Maddie's smiling face punctuated the text: "Where are you?"

"Just taking a walk."

"????" She texted back.

Before he could reply he heard a distant rumble. Dime-sized drops hit the dusty trail. Looking up he noticed the dark clouds that had rolled in while he was lost in his thoughts. Turning he jogged back toward the courtyard. By the time he reached the front door the sky had opened up in a downpour. Well, the weather agrees with my mood, he thought, as he headed for fourth period.

The clouds hadn't emptied by the time school let out, so soccer practice was cancelled. Brett grabbed his backpack from his locker and made a quick exit out the side door toward the parking lot. Pulling out of the school he didn't make his usual left. He pointed his car east and headed toward White Haven Memorial Park. It had been several weeks since he had been to the cemetery. He needed to be close to Jess. Sitting by her gravesite seemed like the place to be.

The rain was still coming down when he pulled into White Haven. The manicured lawns were dotted with flat bronze memorials. Brett wound his car past the expansive lawns toward the nature trail where Jessica's remains were resting among the trees. He pulled into the empty lot, grabbed his jacket from the back seat and headed toward the trail into the forest. Slipping on the windbreaker, he pulled the hood over his dark hair and stuffed his hands into his jean pockets.

He remembered the day that they came here to make arrangements for Jessica's burial. His parents wanted a traditional plot. He had argued with them that Jessica would've wanted a green burial. She was always harping on being "eco-friendly". In the end, he had convinced his parents after they had toured the trail through the tall pines and babbling brooks. The trail was lined with memorial rocks. It just seemed like the kind of place Jess would want to be.

When he located the rock with Jessica's name on it, he plopped down beside it oblivious to the wet ground. Rubbing his hand over the bronze plaque he read the inscription memorializing her short life. "Because she cared," was all it read. It summed up everything he knew and loved about his sister.

Tears mixed with the rain on his face. "Jess, tell me, what was it like there? I want to know everything about what you did, where you went, the people you met. I miss our talks, I miss how excited you were about your adventure. I miss sitting on the couch with you, eating popcorn and watching TV. I miss hiding your things and hearing your laugh when you found them. You know, I only hid them so I could hear you laugh. I loved your laugh. I miss everything about you. Jess, I'm so sorry, so, so sorry. If only I could bring you back."

Brett ran out of tears the same time the clouds ran out of raindrops. A shiver raced up his spine. He realized he was soaking wet.

"Gotta go, Jess. Mom will worry. I promise I'll come back soon." He really wanted to keep that vow.

CHAPTER 8

Friday night's home game was against Allendale's longtime rival, Bloomfield Wildcats. Both teams were coming into the match undefeated, so tension was high.

Coach Bronson had continued to focus in practice on making smart runs and being there for the rebound goal. So, Brett following his usual ritual, envisioned himself making those unexpected finishes. He wanted to show his coach that he could be that well-rounded player and apply the skills they had been drilling over the past few weeks.

Entering the field, the team was greeted by the wave of blue and white. The stands were packed, the cheers were deafening. Brett did a once over and saw Maddie sitting with his parents. To his surprise, he saw the Syracuse scouts already settled in the stands. Wow, coach didn't mention they would be here tonight he thought.

"Alright guys, gather round," Coach Bronson couldn't contain his own excitement. "Let's get this game off to a good start, remember what we've drilled and have fun!"

The ref called the captains to center field. Brett still wasn't used to Rasheed standing there with him but brushed the negative vibes from his mind. Stay positive he reminded himself, I need this guy's misses to make my goals.

"I want a good clean game," the ref gave his regular pregame reminders regarding good sportsmanship. "Away team gets the call."

Watching the coin whirl through the air the Wildcat's captain called, "Heads!" Falling to the shorn grass between them, everyone leaned in as the coin took a bounce and landed tails up.

"Alright," clapped Brett running to the sidelines. The team piled their hands in a pyramid and let out the traditional "OOWWWW!"

Lining up on the centerline, Brett studied Rasheed. The intensity on his face reminded Brett of the conviction he often saw in his sister, Jess.

Rasheed noticing Brett's stare offered encouragement. "Let's do this! The first goal is yours!" Brett caught off guard, wondered what he meant by that but brushed it off. Don't be distracted he thought.

The ref's whistle sounded the start of the game. Brett tapped the ball to Rasheed who used his quick footwork to carry it past the midfielders and into the penalty area. Brett, on the outside right, was ready for the run if the ball was deflected, but Rasheed didn't take the shot. Instead he slowed the game and passed the ball back to the midfielder, who sent it around to the left forward.

Why didn't he take the shot thought Brett, he could've easily beat that defender for the score? Keeping his head in the game, Brett watched as the left forward set up for the cross. Brett and Rasheed were both anticipating the finish but a Wildcat defender made a brilliant tackle and stole the ball. The Wolves were now on the defense.

Brett and Rasheed turned and raced toward center field as the Allendale defenders met their first challenge. The Bloomfield center forward didn't waste any time bringing the ball into the Wolves defensive end. He took the shot but there was no force in the boot, the blue and white goalie easily nabbed the ball.

"Oohhhh," the stands reacted to the miss.

"Settle down," yelled Coach Bronson, "maintain possession now, guys."

The Allendale fullback received the ball from the goalie and took a second to let the team organize. The forwards were making space, trying to shake the orange and black defenders. The team played smart and with easy give and goes worked the ball back into their offensive half. Rasheed had the ball and headed to the right sideline. He danced past the defender remaining in full control. He was in scoring range.

What is he doing thought Brett? Heading for the space opened by Rasheed, he moved to the center of the field right in front of the goal. He saw Rasheed plant his foot and reel back to take the shot. Brett focused on making the run for the finish in case Rasheed missed. But Rasheed didn't aim it at the goal, he passed it across the field ricocheting it off of a defender. Brett was in the right spot when the ball came off the black socks and had an easy tap into the net behind the goalie.

The stands erupted, the team rushed up to Brett slapping his back and high-fiving one another. Brett felt the sweet success of finding the net. He looked for Rasheed and saw him standing by the sidelines. Rasheed pointed at him and mouthed, "Told you!"

How did he do that, did he do that on purpose wondered Brett. He felt a new respect for Rasheed's ball control. It truly seemed as if he had set up that shot for Brett. Looking over at Coach Bronson, he saw him with his hands on his hips, laughing and shaking his head in disbelief.

Coming to the center line, Brett and Rasheed exchanged a fist bump.

"Thanks," Brett offered. Rasheed nodded briefly, then the pregame intensity returned to his face.

"My turn now," was his only response.

But the Wildcats were charged up and didn't waste any time getting the ball within scoring range. The outside fullback made an error in judgment when the Bloomfield forward faked to the right. Smoking the defender, the Wildcat was rewarded with an easy cross that was picture perfect. Charging the ball, the center forward planted it squarely into the net. It was a blur flying past the Allendale goalie. Retrieving it from the net he shook his head wondering what had just happened.

The fans for both sides were on their feet, it was going to be a hotly contested match at this rate. As the game progressed, the defenders for both teams fought to keep the ball from the attacking forwards. The remainder of the half was brutal, with both teams failing to find the reward of a goal.

At the whistle, the score was still 1-1. Both teams headed for their lockers drenched in sweat and feeling the frustration of the deadlock. Brett glanced into the stands while leaving the field. The Syracuse scouts had already left. Just one more concern to add to my list, he thought.

The Wildcats had the ball as the second half started. They had returned to the field fired up and didn't waste any time getting into scoring position. The Allendale goalie was caught flat-footed for a brief moment. Bloomfield's center forward took advantage of the situation and fired the ball like a bullet shot into the net.

"Aahhhh," disappointment reverberated through the Allendale stands. Now the Wolves had to play catch up. The team regrouped in center field.

"Alright guys. Let's tighten up the defense and control the ball." Brett barked encouragement to his teammates. As the players moved into position on the field he remembered the first shot that Rasheed didn't take. I won't forgive him if that cost us the game he thought.

The next twenty minutes were grueling, back and forth, close misses, brilliant saves, but the clock was ticking and the score was still 2-1, favoring Bloomfield.

With ten minutes left, Rasheed trapped the ball that was punted to him by their goalie. Brett saw him kick into overdrive and tried to keep pace racing up the sideline. Shaking each defender Rasheed put on his best show ever of fabulous footwork, bringing the ball into scoring range. Brett made ready for the rebound but it wasn't necessary. Rasheed fainted left drawing the fullback and goalie with him and gently finessed the ball into the right corner of the goal. The fans came to their feet in unison, followed by an earsplitting roar.

"Alright guys, we got this!" Brett gathered his team at centerfield as Rasheed was given skin around the huddle. "Remember the drill," Brett was trying to get the team to focus but he looked directly at Rasheed who nodded in agreement.

Minutes were ticking away, both teams were giving it their all. Only one team was going home "undefeated" tonight. With a minute thirty to play, Allendale got a lucky break when a Wildcat player got called for tackling Rasheed from behind. The team lined up as he prepared for the direct kick. It would normally be an easy shot for him to make but there was a sea of orange and black barricading the target. Blue and white players were scattered among the defenders, anticipating the rebound.

Brett stood to the right of the goal, waiting for the whistle. He took a deep breath. Closing his eyes, he envisioned his foot kissing the ball and tapping it into the corner behind the goalie.

The ref signaled the restart of play as Rasheed put the finishing touches on centering up the ball. With thirty seconds left on the clock, Rasheed let loose with full force on the orb planted in the grass. Brett tracked the ball as it sailed toward the goal. He started his run as the goalie reached up to bat the ball out of the air. As if in slow motion, Brett watched the ball come his direction and land directly at his feet. The goalie was stunned. Brett gave an ever so gentle tap and the ball rolled into the goal like a billiard finding its pocket, exactly how he had envisioned it. The seconds ticked off, the ref blew the whistle, then pandemonium broke loose.

Brett found himself squeezed between teammates, students and parents as they raced to the field to celebrate the 3-2 victory. Looking over the ocean of heads he saw Rasheed standing outside the crowd. Pointing to get his attention, Brett pounded his fist to his chest in gratitude.

#####

From the ruckus in the locker room one would think they had just won the World Cup. The Allendale players had earned bragging rights and they weren't going to let the Wildcats forget it. Gathering his gear, Brett made for the exit and was greeted by a flood of fans. Pushing his way through the crowd, he saw Maddie waiting anxiously by his car.

"Geno's?" It was time to celebrate!

"Sure, after that game I need a victory pizza." Brett felt like his old self as he grabbed her in his arms and swung her around.

"Jump in, the 'Stang is your chariot tonight!" He bowed as he opened the door, Maddie planted a kiss on his cheek. This all feels so good he thought.

By the time they got to Geno's it was standing room only. Just inside the door they scanned the crowd and saw most of the team surrounding a table in the back.

"Hey, make way for the star," someone yelled as Brett, dragging Maddie, weaved through the maze of people and chairs. Brett was offered a chair at the head of the table. Grabbing a vacant seat, he pulled it over for Maddie.

"That's my cha..." The sophomore stopped mid-sentence when he saw Brett. "That's ok, it's all yours," he said as he moved off into the crowd.

Surveying all the people, Brett was wondering how long it was going to take to get food, when a hot, steaming, meat-lover's pizza was plopped in front of him.

"On the house!" exclaimed Jake, "Tonight you're wish is my command."

Brett was taking in all the revelry and enjoying the limelight. His eyes danced around the room and he noticed Rasheed sitting two tables over with a group of girls.

"What's he doing here?" He nudged Maddie and directed her attention to the huddle of happy faces.

"Brett, he's part of the team and part of our school. What do you have against him?" She didn't want to ruin the celebrating but didn't understand Brett's resistance to this guy.

"Nothing," he said chomping into a spicy piece of pizza. Pulling at the string of cheese he kept an eye on Rasheed. He sure is having a good time Brett thought, he acts like he belongs here.

"So, what do you think, Brett...Brett?" Maddie interrupted his thoughts.

"What were you saying?" Brett snapped out of his private world. Before she could answer Rasheed got up and headed their way. In a few short steps, he was standing in front of them.

"Join us, please," Maddie was quick to offer him a seat. Before Brett could comment Rasheed plopped down beside them.

Maddie and Rasheed got into a quick conversation and Brett eyed them with suspicion as they chatted like long lost friends. He downed another piece of pizza listening to their idle chit-chat. Despite the victory, he had a bone to pick with Rasheed.

"So, I have a question?" Brett interrupted the conversation causing them both to stop short. They turned in unison to look at him and saw that all cheer had left his face. The conversation got serious.

"I want to know what you were doing?" Brett sounded like an interrogation officer. His eyes boring holes into Rasheed's deepest thoughts.

"I am not sure what you are referring too." Rasheed's puzzlement matched Maddie's confusion.

"Your first attack on the goal, you didn't take the shot. I want to know why?"

"I told you the first goal was yours." Rasheed's ears turned red. There was an awkward pause as Brett tried to process what this meant.

"You were sacrificing a score so I could get the first point on the board?" Brett slouched in his chair, a statue of bewilderment.

"Yes, I know you are the leader of the team and I don't want to take your place away from you."

Brett could not believe his ears. Is this guy feeling sorry for me he wondered? I don't need his pity. Contemplating Rasheed's answer a moment more, Brett went from incomprehension to rage. He turned on Rasheed and cut loose.

"You could have sacrificed the whole game playing around like that. We barely won as it was! You aren't playing for the team. What are you doing here anyway?" Maddie grabbed his arm and Brett stopped to catch his breath. The place had gone quiet and all eyes were on their table.

"What!" The full force of his anger was aimed at her.

"I think we should go." She was looking for an escape from the embarrassing situation.

"I'm going to finish my pizza!" Sulking, Brett sat back and grabbed another slice, catching the dangling cheese with his tongue.

"Let's see if your pizza is ready," Maddie got up, offering Rasheed a graceful exit. Studying Brett's face, Rasheed couldn't figure out what he had done wrong.

"Come on," Maddie grabbed his hand and they maneuvered their way to the counter.

They took his cheese pizza to a table that had just emptied and she sat with him while he dug in. The crowd had returned to its normal clamor. Maddie studied Rasheed as he worked his way through the pieces. All teenage boys eat with the same ferocity she thought.

When he finished, he wiped his face and folded the napkin neatly. "What was my error?"

Maddie shrugged, "Brett's going through a lot of stuff, I'm not sure."

Rasheed's eyes ventured from her, at the same moment Maddie felt the presence of someone behind her.

"You don't need to talk about my problems." No need to look, she knew who had made the snide comment.

"I think you should get a ride," Brett snapped as he turned away. Maddie sat stunned, as she watched the back of his Allendale jacket exit Geno's.

"My aunt will take you home," Rasheed offered as a tear rolled down her cheek.

"You're sweet, but I'll call my dad. He always tells me he will come get me, no matter what, no questions." She picked up her phone and headed for the door.

CHAPTER 9

Brett woke the next morning still in the jeans and t-shirt he had worn to Geno's. Shaking the morning fog from his head he remembered the victory and a feeling of contentment came over him as he pulled the covers back over his head. Seconds later he bolted upright and grabbed his phone.

Geez, what did I do he thought. He pounded out a text and shot it off to Maddie. "We need to talk. Sorry for ditching you last night."

Urgently pacing his room, he glanced at his phone every few minutes in hopes that by some magic an answer would relieve his anxiety. I've got to do something, this is making me crazy, he thought. Grabbing a clean shirt and his jeans he made for the shower. With warm water washing over him, he relived the scene at Geno's. The stark expression on Maddie's face was etched on his mind's eye. He couldn't shake the feeling that he had wrecked their relationship. Why can't I tame this rage inside me he wondered?

Stepping from the shower, his body red as a lobster from a pot, he quickly dressed and raced to check his phone. Drying the last drops from his hair, he saw there was still no reply. That's not like her he thought, I've got to do something.

Racing down the steps, he grabbed his jacket, key ring and snatched a banana from the bottomless fruit bowl on the counter.

His mom stepping into the kitchen, saw the anguish on his face. "What's up, Brett?"

"Gotta go," was all he replied as he headed for the door.

"Where are you taking off to in such a hurry?"

"The stables!"

"Breakfast?"

"Got some," he offered up the banana to appease her motherly concern. Before she could press the conversation further, he pulled the door shut and raced to his car. She's gotta be there he thought as he backed the car from the drive and headed toward Lehman's.

As Brett pulled into the lane at the stables, the sun was sparkling off the frost-covered grass like a thousand diamonds shimmering on a chandelier. Fall was rapidly waning. The cold nipped at his ears as he stepped from the car. Pulling up his jacket's suede collar he looked like a turtle retreating into his shell. He stuffed his hands into the fleece-lined pockets and surveyed the lot searching for Maddie's plum-colored Honda. The gravel parking was virtually empty, so it only took a moment for him to spot her wheels. Good, now what can I do to make it up to her he thought.

The stones crunched beneath his Timberland hikers as he headed for the stable doors. As always, Bruno spotted him the minute he stepped through the doorway and wasted no time sharing his usual greeting of sloppy kisses.

"Good to see you too ol' boy," said Brett pulling his hands from their warm hibernation. He bent down to give Bruno a thorough rubdown.

"She's here, right?" He asked the dog as if expecting a full rundown on Maddie's mood. The chocolate lab nuzzled Brett's neck and licked at his ears.

"Ok, ok, I hope she's feeling friendly too." Brett stood up. Taking a deep breath, he summoned up his courage as he headed toward Midnight's stall. Bruno followed him down the aisle and took up post outside the door as if he knew Brett needed the moral support.

Peering around the corner of the stall, he saw Maddie hard at work on Midnight's coat. The savage strokes she landed with the dandy brush made Brett feel guilty. Sorry she's taking it out on you, he thought, as Midnight winced away from the pressure of the bristles.

"You didn't answer my text." It was feeble but it was all he could think to say.

She stopped mid-stroke and gave Brett a hard glare, then went back to the task at hand. No words were spoken, Brett knew he was in trouble.

"Would it help if I said I was sorry?"

A second evil glare answered that question. She continued brushing Midnight, leaving the air between them electrically charged.

Brett stepped into the stall and gently caressed the white blaze on Midnight's muzzle. Watching Maddie, he realized he had never seen her like this before. I've definitely gone too far he thought, I hope there is a way back into her good graces.

"Look Maddie, can you stop for a moment so we can talk?" He hated pleading but had no choice.

She threw down the brush and crossed her arms. Hip propped against the tack box she waited for Brett to continue. Her somber expression told all.

"I'm really sorry," he started. There was still no response, just that cold stare. "You have a right to be upset, I get it, but I just don't know what is happening with me. One moment I think everything is fine and the next moment my world is spinning."

Maddie's gaze softened slightly.

"My senior year is not going how I thought it would. Everything is a jumble and I can't sort it out. You and soccer are the only two things that make any sense to me, but right now I can't even keep that straight." Brett sighed, just getting that out somehow untangled a small piece of the twisted twine that were his thoughts.

Maddie wrapped her arms around him and the block of ice inside of her melted. The floodgates opened and a torrent streamed down her cheeks. Using a towel Brett found in the tack box, he dabbed at her tears. After a few minutes, Maddie composed herself and grabbed Brett's hand pulling him to have a seat beside her on the box. Brett studied her bright blue eyes that shimmered with puddles of sorrow. He knew how Maddie operated, so he waited patiently while she gathered her thoughts.

"Brett, I know you are having a hard time. I just want to help you. But I can't understand why you are so angry with Rasheed. He's a really nice guy and he is struggling to belong here, he needs help too." She paused for a moment as if thinking over whether she really wanted to say what she thought. Taking a deep breath, she plunged forward as if diving into the darkest depths.

"Rasheed didn't kill Jessica!" There, she said it!

Brett was stunned, the tangled web in his mind snagged all reason. He lost hold of the safety lines he was holding onto only moments ago. Not wanting to make matters worse, he held his tongue. Maddie was staring hard at him, looking for some sort of response.

"I'm always here to help," she continued. "But you need to figure this out. You know, Ms. Michaels told me she offered to help too."

"Are you talking to everyone about my problems?" Brett was spiraling out of control...again.

"No Brett, just know that people care." She gently brushed back his hair. She could see the hurt in his eyes. Her heart ached for him.

Not knowing what to say or do, he got up and headed out the stall door.

"Brett..." He didn't stop. She watched him walk down the aisle and head toward his car. Bruno nuzzled against her, she squatted and buried her face in the soft nap of his neck. The floodgates let loose again.

#####

There was only one place to retreat to, so Brett turned in the direction of Corbett's Glen. Pulling into the empty lot, Brett shut off his car and laid his head back. Squeezing his eyes tightly closed trying to hold back the tears that were beckoning. He recalled the nightmare that still haunted him. Rasheed holding the AK-47 that had killed Jessica.

How does Maddie do it he wondered, it's as if she is in my head. She knows me better than I know myself. It is so easy to lay all of the blame for Jessica's death at Rasheed's feet, it helps relieve some of my own guilt, he thought. But none of it brings Jess back. He couldn't contain his grief any longer, tears streamed down his face.

When his anguish subsided, he slid from his car, bundled up in his jacket and headed for the falls. The sound of his single footsteps crunching through the crumpled leaves, made him long for Gramps. If only I had your direction he thought. Why can't I like him, he's done nothing to me.

"Gramps...answer me," he shouted into the wind.

In a flash, a picture popped into his mind's eye. It was as if his Grandpa had tapped him on the shoulder. Brett was transported back to fifth grade, when Kaleb transferred to Allendale. Every night Brett came home with another complaint about Kaleb's shenanigans, he was always stealing the show.

This went on for weeks, Kaleb this, Kaleb that. One-night Gramps looked him square in the face and asked, "What do you like about Kaleb?"

The question had stopped Brett mid-sentence. He realized that he wasn't giving the guy a chance.

"Well?" Gramps had never let him off the hook.

Brett took several minutes to turn this over in his head, "He's really good at Super Mario!"

"Ok then, why don't you have him over to play. I'm sure he needs a few friends at a new school." Gramps walked away leaving Brett to work out when they could hook up.

Brett chuckled, that had been the start of a great friendship. Sure, Kaleb still annoyed him sometimes but he was a loyal friend.

Turning Gramps' question over in his head, he looked for something to like about Rasheed. It only took a second to find the answer...soccer! He makes me a much better player thought Brett. I've learned so much watching him handle the ball.

Picking up some stones and heaving them into the falls, Brett resolved to give Rasheed a chance. Plopping the stones, one by one, he thought of the contest he always had with his Grandpa to see who could hit closest to the center rock in the falls.

"I win," he said as he landed one dead center. "Thanks, for hearing me Gramps." He headed back to his car as the sun began to thaw the morning.

Turning his face upward, he was soaking in the warm rays when he heard "My Girl" blaring from the phone he had left in the car. Maddie's ringtone! Trotting to catch the call, he picked it up just as it stopped. He had missed four calls, all from Maddie.

"Oh geez." He felt panic rising inside. He found her name at the top of his "recents". With his finger hovering over her name, a text popped in.

"I didn't want to do it this way, but if you don't want to talk now it's OK. I just think we need to cool it a bit until you can sort things out. :'("

Reading the text, he felt like his heart had been ripped from his chest. What do I do now Gramps, he thought, you never had a chance to give me women advice?

CHAPTER 10

Brett sulked around the house the rest of the weekend. Every text and call to Maddie seemed to fall into a black abyss. By Sunday afternoon he definitely needed a change of scenery so he took off for Geno's, pizza solves so many problems.

He was greeted by his favorite smell as he stepped through the door, garlic! Catching Jake's eye, he ordered the regular. With a nod Jake went to work. Brett did a quick once over to see who might be hanging out. He was shocked to see Rasheed sitting alone at a booth in the back. OK, now's as good a time as any he thought. He sauntered over to the table and waited quietly, unnoticed for a moment.

Brett took a deep breath, "Mind if I join you?" He noted the surprise on Rasheed's face.

"Please do sit," Rasheed didn't even hesitate at his invitation.

They sat staring at one another, Brett couldn't find the words to start. Rasheed broke the silence, "Great game, Friday."

"Yeah, about that...I need to apologize for my behavior after the game." Brett was struggling with what to say, he wasn't used to "eating crow".

"No need, I understand your upset. You wanted to be sure the team won. I was trying not to...how do you say it," Rasheed hesitated, trying to find the right words, "I don't want to steal your show."

"Yeah, it was still not ok...how I treated you." Each minute seemed like an eternity. Gosh how do I do this he thought fidgeting with his keys. Jake showed up with the pizza and sat it between them. Glancing between the two boys, he felt like he had interrupted a lover's spat.

"Come on, eat up while it's hot," Jake was only happy when hungry boys were eating.

"Please have some," offered Brett, handing Rasheed the spatula.

"Thank you," Rasheed grabbed a piece of the meat lovers and tore into it.

"Hey, did you have pizza in Afghanistan?" Brett felt a

new curiosity regarding Rasheed.

"Oh no, I learned about it when I was young in England, before we moved for my father's job. I like American pizza best though," he snatched up a pepperoni that had landed on his plate, popping it into his mouth.

The minutes ticked by while they both downed a couple of pieces chasing them with their sodas. Brett still felt like he was on thin ice but was determined to make a good show of trying to like Rasheed. Thinking back to yesterday at Corbett's Glen he turned to the one subject they shared a love for, soccer.

"So, where did you learn to play like you do," Brett felt a calm rush over him. He could talk to anyone about soccer.

"My father played for his college and some semi-pro in England, I learned so much about the game from him." Brett could see how proud Rasheed was of his father.

"Hey, my dad played college ball too, American football that is. He doesn't know much about soccer but he taught me about hard work." They were on a common ground now, so it was getting easier to talk.

Before long they had their heads together using the table condiments to work out plays. They hardly noticed when Jake came by and cleared the empty plates.

Minutes later, a refill of drinks showed up. They thanked Jake and went back to the field mocked up between them.

They were dragged from their conversation when Brett's phone jangled with a text. Picking it up he saw that his mom was checking on him. *"Are you going to be on time for dinner?"*

It was her sweet way of trying to find out where he was. He realized he hadn't told her where he was going. She has a right to worry he thought, she's trying to deal with Jess's death too.

"Be there soon," he shot back.

"Gotta go," he said as he slid from the booth. "This was great," he offered with all sincerity.

"Thank you kindly for sharing your pizza," Rasheed slipped back into his polite prose.

"Yeah," when Brett offered a fist bump, Rasheed was taken back at first, then realized what he was doing. A huge smile swept across his face as their knuckles met.

Brett heading across the restaurant, turned as he reached the door. "See you tomorrow," he offered. Rasheed gave him a thumbs-up. Well, we might Americanize him some day he chuckled. And, I might get a friend out of it too he thought.

As Brett jumped into his car, he realized he hadn't

thought of Maddie for the past two hours. Well, I still have soccer in my life.

#####

On Monday morning, Brett dropped into his normal seat in the back of American Government. He was anxiously waiting for Maddie, maybe he could get a few words in with her before class started. Patiently watching the door, his heart skipped a beat when he saw her step into the room.

Without looking his way, she plopped down in the first seat by the door. She didn't acknowledge the greetings sent her way as other kids arrived. This is so unlike her Brett thought, she always talks to everyone. What have I done?

The class settled in their seats when the bell went off. Whoops and hollers followed a brief announcement congratulating the team on Friday's win. Brett noticed Maddie stoically focused on the wall in front of her.

"Ok class, get out your 'Story of Human Rights' booklets, we are going to look at articles 18 and 19 today. Take a moment to read those summaries and then we'll watch the video clips. Today we are going to look at freedom of thought and freedom of religion, two concepts that are the basis of our own constitution and the reason so many people have immigrated to the US since our country was founded." Ms. Michaels spoke with passion.

Unfortunately, Brett was lost in a daze. The sound of Ms. Michaels voice droned on in the background, but he couldn't concentrate on her words. He was experiencing a new anguish, heartbreak. The bell jerked him from his bewilderment. Class was already over? Where had the hour gone? He felt like he was in a time warp.

Jumping from his seat, he rushed out the door trying to catch up with Maddie. He focused on her blond ponytail bobbing back and forth as she dodged fellow students in the hall. I've gotta catch her, I need to explain...what? He had no idea what he was going to explain, he just needed to say something. Before he could catch up with her, she was swallowed by the mob of students pin-balling off one another to their next class.

It seemed she was evading him all day. When she didn't show up at lunch everyone avoided asking the obvious questions. Brett felt like he was the huge elephant in the room that no one wanted to talk about.

At the day's final bell, he rushed to his locker and grabbed his phone. No messages. He sent her a quick plea, *"Can we at least talk for a few minutes?"* He was hoping he could think of something that would change her mind. As he headed to the soccer field, he checked for an answer every few minutes. Maybe they could meet after practice.

Reaching the field, Coach Bronson was already rounding up the team. He reluctantly tucked the phone in his bag. Time to concentrate on soccer, at least it will give me a few moments of distraction he thought. Throwing his ball to his feet he dribbled toward the team.

"Alright guys, we have two more season games and if we come out of those unscathed we will be looking at sectionals." The roar that followed could have woken the dead.

"Ok, ok," it took Coach a few minutes to settle the guys down. "This is getting exciting, but we've still got some work to do. Let's get started with some warm-up ball touches."

The team got down to business. Rasheed worked his way toward Brett and before long they were knocking the ball between themselves. There seemed to be a new wave length between them, they instinctively knew what the other guy was going to do. Coach Bronson watched in amazement, pleased that his star players were finally gelling.

As always, when Brett was on the soccer field the rest of the world disappeared. It wasn't until practice was over that he thought about Maddie. First thing he did was dig in his bag for his phone. He stopped short when he saw the blank screen...man, nothing! What do I do he wondered? I never thought I would lose Maddie.

His head buried in his hands, he sunk to the bench beside his bag. He felt as if his heart was breaking into a million tiny pieces. He had no idea how to fix it.

Coach Bronson was gathering up the soccer supplies still lying around the field. Seeing Brett, he wandered over and quietly sat down.

"What's happening?" he murmured. Brett jolted, so lost in his thoughts he hadn't noticed Coach beside him.

"Oh, uhh..." Before he could decide what to say Coach Bronson uttered one word, "Maddie?"

Brett studied his coach's face, trying to figure out how he knew.

Before he could say anything, coach continued, "It was on the teacher's hotline that something was up between you two."

Brett was torn, he didn't know whether to give him the whole scene or blow it off as nothing. How do you explain these things he wondered? Coach Bronson sat patiently waiting for Brett to respond.

Taking the leap, Brett blurted out, "Last Friday after the game, I messed up. I left her at Geno's," he mumbled the last part, as if ashamed of his behavior. "Now she wants to take some time off, if you know what I mean." He purposely avoided getting into the scene at the stable.

"Oh, I see." Coach paused, "would you like some women advice?" He was peering wisely over his glasses, trying not to push too hard.

"Sure, it's one thing Gramps never got a chance to explain to me. I can usually find some of his wisdom floating around in my brain, but I'm just blank on women." Brett was shaking his head as if rattling dice and betting. Hoping with the next toss, a solution would turn up.

"You have crossed the line all men have to jump over if they want to keep their lady happy. It's hard to live with them, but even harder to live without them." Coach let out a brief chuckle as if he was remembering his first stab at wooing a lady.

"I'm not sure I can replace your grandfather, but I can give you two things I've learned throughout my years. First, give her some space to work it out. Women have to think these things over for a while." Coach seemed very certain on that point.

"How long?" There was total bewilderment in Brett's voice.

"Can't say, it's not one of those things that has a definitive end." Coach shrugged.

What kind of answer is that thought Brett.

"It's been three days already, this is torture!" Brett

was trying to figure out how he would make it through another day feeling like this but gave up.

"What else?" He hoped the next piece of advice would hold the ultimate answer to end his torment.

"Second, flowers!" Coach Bronson gave him a broad smile.

Brett stared hard at him to be sure he was serious.

Coach, seeing the surprise on Brett's face continued, "Honest, works every time. Women love to get flowers. It melts their heart."

Brett started to chuckle, remembering all the times his dad had come home carrying his mom's favorite bouquet. She had reacted exactly as coach said. Whatever was up between them had always seemed to vanish when his mom smelled lilacs, as if the aroma itself was a magic potion.

Brett stood up and grabbed his soccer bag, "Men should be given some kind of how-to book on dealing with women. How are we supposed to know this stuff?"

"Trial and error son, trial and error."

"That's rough." Brett was trying to process exactly what that would entail. "Well," he paused, "thanks Coach, I should get going." Racing toward his car, Brett was already searching his phone for the nearest florist. I hope it's that easy he thought.

Sitting behind the wheel, he searched through the multitude of bouquets offered on line. He was trying to decide what Maddie would like best. After looking at page after page of every kind of flower and arrangement imaginable, he decided simple was better and ordered a single long-stem, red rose. The site said that a red rose means "I love you". There wasn't anything else he could think to say so he just signed it "Brett". He made arrangements to have it sent immediately, then started his car and headed toward home.

After dinner, he received a short text, his hand was shaking as he grabbed his phone hoping it was from Maddie. *"Thank you,"* was all it said. Well, it's a response he thought. What do I do now? Maybe I should just give her some time. Shaking his head, he headed for bed. This "trial and error" stuff is rough he thought, turning out the lights.

CHAPTER 11

The next two weeks were an emotional roller coaster for Brett. He and Rasheed had gotten in sync on the field and they were an unstoppable duo. With both of them being an ominous scoring threat, the defenders from the opposing teams couldn't decide who to mark when. The Wolves easily pulled off the last two wins needed to put them in the Section V Championship. The school was buzzing with excitement over the upcoming game.

Brett got through the school days with Maddie behaving sociably to him when others were around, but overall, she avoided any personal conversations. He felt at a loss in the "women" arena. He was following Coach Bronson's advice and giving her time, but he found the waiting game was pure anguish.

He was missing Jessica more than ever. She was his go-to person when things weren't going right. She had always shared his victories and his losses like they were her own. He was feeling a huge void in so many areas of his life. The only bright spot was soccer.

#####

The Wolves would be taking on Bishop Kearney Kings for the Section V Championship. The Kings had several Sectional and State titles to their credit. This was Allendale's first attempt at a soccer title, it was easy for the players to feel intimidated coming into the game as the underdog. Coach Bronson spent the week fine tuning the special plays, any advantage on corner kicks, throw ins or even PK's could mean the difference in the outcome of the game.

Brett tried to stay focused. Coach assured him the Syracuse scouts would be at the game. In his mind his entire future was hanging on this match.

It seemed like the whole school and then some turned out for the big game. The night was brisk but Brett thought it was the perfect temperature to play. As the King's players, dressed in red and gold, were introduced he scanned the crowd. It only took him a few minutes to spot the scouts, they always seemed to gravitate to the same area of the stands. He found his parents among the sea of blue and white, but this time Maddie wasn't sitting with them.

He didn't have time to search for her as the emcee started announcing the Allendale player's. A wild roar went up when his name was called, the stomping in the stands sounded like a herd of wild buffalo. There was an equally loud acknowledgement when the announcer called Rasheed's name. He went down the line of players, high-fiving each teammate. When he got to Brett, he stopped for a moment and looked him square in the eye.

"Let's do this!" Rasheed exclaimed. Brett grabbed him in a wild embrace, the fans went crazy. Everyone knew they were the reason the team had gotten this far. The crowd and teams settled briefly for the National Anthem, but at the last note the madness started where it had left off.

Brett and Rasheed joined the captains from the Kings team and tried to concentrate on the instructions the ref was reeling off. Their excitement was hard to contain. Allendale won the toss and chose to kickoff. They headed to the sidelines and huddled up, eager to start.

Coach Bronson offered his encouragement, "We've come a long way this year, whatever happens tonight, you guys are all champs. Let's have some fun!" His words were followed by the traditional cheer, the fans howling in unison.

As the teams took the field, Brett recognized the familiar intensity on Rasheed's face that meant he was "in his zone". At the whistle, Rasheed tapped the ball forward ever so slightly toward Brett. Brett flicked it to the right and threaded it through the oncoming BK players. He carried it to the outside and up the line. Scanning the field, he saw Rasheed moving toward the space at the top of the penalty box and set his foot for the cross. Before he could get it off a King's defender stepped in and won the ball with a sound stick. The BK players had obviously been watching game films. Rasheed had two defenders on him and another had cornered Brett in an effort to shut down the duo.

This is going to be a tough one thought Brett, as he chased down the defender that had nabbed the ball. The King's offense didn't waste any time opening up space and passed the ball from player to player with precision. They had the first shot on goal, but the Wolves goalie made an easy catch. Clutching the ball, he stopped for a moment to let the team regroup and move into position.

He gave the ball a light punt, which Rasheed caught on his chest and effortlessly dropped to his feet. Wasting no time, he blasted past the Kings offense. Brett was ready for the give and go, hoping to give Rasheed the opportunity to gain ground and get into scoring range. But Rasheed was double teamed again, so instead of returning the ball Brett slowed down and dropped it back to a center fielder. He saw Rasheed trying to shake the defenders.

A King's mid-fielder took advantage of the slow in tempo, stepped in and snatched the ball. He had it only for a few taps and was contested by a Wolves defender who won the ball with a good stick, then ended up chasing it out of bounds.

Brett was oblivious to the clamor of the crowd, he was concentrating on how he and Rasheed could put some passes together to find the back of the net. Back and forth the ball went. Fast attacks, tight defense, brilliant saves by both goalies. Neither team finding a way to score. The half ended 0-0. The crowd was wound tighter than a clock. An uproarious cheer followed the teams into the lockers.

Leaving the field, Brett scanned the stands. The scouts were still there, he was looking for disappointment on their faces. Their heads were together as they seemed to be jotting notes on their tablet. Shaking them from his attention, he headed for the locker.

He lagged behind the rest of the team, waiting for Coach Bronson to catch up.

"Remember our first game, Coach?" Brett was working on a strategy to hopefully confuse the King's defenders.

"Yeah Brett, let's do it!" Coach patted him on the shoulder as they entered the locker, "You're thinking like a coach now, heh?"

Tension was high as the players returned to the field. Rasheed had changed places with the center half, hoping that another offensive player in the box would splint the defenders and get points on the board for Allendale.

The Kings had first possession and didn't waste any time on their attack. The centerfielder sent a long pass to the right forward who trapped it and then fired a shot from outside the penalty box. The ball whizzed past the goalie and racketed around in the back of the net. Thunder erupted from the BK stands.

"Let's get it back," commanded Brett, as the team lined up for their first run in the second half. He saw the King's players switching positions trying to figure out how to cover both Rasheed and the new forward coming at them.

The ball was served up to Brett, who wasted no time carrying it up the line. Without delay, he crossed it to their forward who got off a great shot, but it was deflected by the goalie. Rasheed saw his chance. The defenders saw him coming but were a step behind. Charging in from the top of the penalty box, he trapped the ball, tapped it with his right foot and then fired a left-footed rocket that stunned everyone including

Brett. The Allendale fans went wild as the ball blazed into the net. New game, 1-1. It was Rasheed's way of saying the game wasn't over yet.

"I didn't know you were left footed," Brett declared as he congratulated Rasheed.

"You have to keep all your options open!" Rasheed was beaming as they lined up for the kick off.

Now Brett was really fired up. The ref blew the whistle and a red jersey headed his way trying to dance past him. Brett read the player's fake and swiped the ball. Racing up the sideline he saw a blue and white jersey racing toward the back corner of the goal. Brett fired the ball across the field and his teammate got off a shot. Unfortunately, it ricocheted off the top bar. The goal post can be your friend or your enemy thought Brett.

"Ohhhh!" The stands on both sides of the field were equally excited about the near miss.

The Kings goalie punted the ball toward centerfield. Rasheed correctly calculated its trajectory and stepped in, easily winning the ball. The Allendale players were ablaze. They wasted no time attacking the goal again. This time Rasheed fired a high shot, the goalie stretched and punched it over the bar.

The fans were on their feet, the clock was ticking. Who was going to take the Sectional title?

The Kings players were clearly rattled. They had failed to get any offense going since their first score. The change in the Allendale lineup confused the defenders who were scrambling to protect the goal. The BK goalie was getting a workout. The Wolves fired ball after ball at him but were unable to reap the reward. He was King's defensive hero as he repeatedly stopped Allendale from putting any more points on the scoreboard.

"Ten, nine, eight, seven…" The whole stadium counted down the final seconds. Rasheed made one last attempt to give Allendale the lead, but BK's goalie easily nabbed the ball and held it for the final count. It was 1-1 at the buzzer.

The tension in the crowd was energizing. Both teams chose five players who lined up for the penalty kicks. It was a highly fought match and the Sectional Championship had come down to which team could put the most PKs in the net.

The first three players on both teams didn't get past the goalies so when the Kings fourth player stepped to the line the score was still 1-1. The Allendale goalie was on his toes and ready. The player shifted left and drew the goalie that way then easily tapped the ball into the right corner of the net. The stands erupted. It was now 2-1 in favor of BK.

Rasheed stepped to the line. Brett saw it on his face that this ball was going in the back of the net. Rasheed rocketed it past the goalie, hitting the upper 90 and making it an even match again. There were two players left to shoot. The Kings star forward and Brett, the game came down to what these two could make happen.

The Kings player came to the line full of confidence. From his attitude, Brett could tell where he was putting the ball. Allendale's goalie was on his toes again, a bit rattled by the last score but clearly keeping his head in the game. He watched as the kicker placed his left foot pointing toward the left corner of the goal, which usually meant the ball was following that path. Leaning his hips to the left, he dove as the orb sailed toward the goal. Catching the ball with the tip of his outstretched glove he knocked it off course, preventing the score.

The Allendale stands went wild, this was their last chance. Brett stepped to the line, took a deep breath to calm his nerves and visualized his motions, mentally reviewing all the points Coach had drilled through the week. He set the ball, then stepping back he tuned out the racket coming from the stands. Turning back toward the goal, he avoided making eye contact with the goalie. He just saw the whole net and the sweet spot he was aiming for. Ok, I've been watching this goalie, he thought, he's quick on his toes but weaker on the left. I'm going lower left. The ref blew the whistle, Brett took four long strides and his foot met the ball precisely as he had practiced. Everything seemed to move in slow motion as the goalie tried to correct his direction at the last minute. He was seconds behind and those seconds were enough for the ball to sail past him into the lower left corner of the goal. Exactly how Brett had envisioned it!

The fans attacked the field with as much ferocity as the players had attacked the game. Brett and Rasheed found themselves in the air above the crowd, riding on their teammate's shoulders. Someone handed them the Sectional trophy and they held it between themselves high in the air. The celebration was timeless! Brett closed his eyes, burning the picture forever in his memory.

#####

The festivities were moved to an impromptu party at Kaleb's house. Everyone congratulated Brett as he strolled through the crowded living room. He listened as person after person relived their version of the final play. Brett felt like he was floating in an alternate reality. He had never experienced this level of happiness and didn't want to come down off the high.

Making his way through the maze of bodies, he finally entered the kitchen where he grabbed a slice of pizza and made for the backyard. There was a bright campfire surrounded by huddles of bodies chattering and laughing. Brett headed for the group and saw Rasheed sitting alone on a log beside the fire.

"Mind if I have a seat?" He paused briefly. Not waiting for an answer, he found a space next to Rasheed. He offered a high five, "Awesome game, man!"

"You were brilliant on that PK. The game could have gone on for another round. Well planned on your part."

Brett felt a bit embarrassed, he knew he wasn't the real star in the game, "Hey, it was a team effort!"

"Yes," was all Rasheed added. There were a few minutes of uncomfortable silence as they both stared into the fire, then Rasheed asked the big question. "What are those white things they're cooking?"

"You mean the marshmallows? You've never had a marshmallow?" Brett chuckled in disbelief.

"What are they, why are they burning them?" Rasheed was clearly confused by this old campfire tradition.

"They're idiots, you don't burn a marshmallow, you lightly toast them." Brett explained as if he was the expert. "Then, when they are cooked just right, you pop them in your mouth. It's like eating a sugar cloud."

Brett had grabbed a stick and pushed two plump marshmallows on the end. He enjoyed teaching

Rasheed something in exchange for all the things he had learned from him on the field.

"How long does this take?" Rasheed watched as Brett slowly rotated the stick like a pig on a spit.

"Let's see," Brett pulled the marshmallows from the fire and gently squeezed them, checking to see if they were done. "Perfection," he said. He presented them to Rasheed as if they were a delicacy.

Rasheed wasted no time gobbling them off the end of the stick. "Wow, that's a sugar fix alright!"

"You don't have them in Afghanistan?" Brett quizzed Rasheed.

"No, most of the sweets my mother allowed us were from dried fruits and nuts. She would probably not be happy with this American marshmallow. But since she is not here, let me cook another one!"

They were both laughing at Rasheed's attempt to get the marshmallow on the stick when Maddie walked up.

"Let me offer congratulations," she said. They both stopped mid-action, staring at her like they had been caught doing something wrong.

Rasheed broke the silence, "Thank you Miss Madison!" He bowed his head as he slipped into his formal tongue.

"Yeah, thanks," said Brett trying to sound relaxed.

"It's good to see you two getting along." She stepped over several sets of legs stretched out next to the fire and sat down beside Rasheed.

"I was teaching him about roasting marshmallows." What a stupid thing to say, he thought. Then, on second thought, he added, "We get along, didn't you see us on the field tonight?"

"Yeah, you guys were great." She was trying to sound cheerful but she had other things on her mind.

"I must excuse myself," Rasheed offered politely. He stood, handing the stick back to Brett. "Good evening Miss Madison." Stuffing his hands in his pockets, he retreated to the house.

Madison slid over closer to Brett.

"Would you like a marshmallow?" Brett was trying to be polite and it was the only thing he could think to say. He had been waiting for what seemed like forever for Maddie to be ready to talk to him. Now all he could think about were stupid marshmallows.

"No..." she hesitated, "It's great you and Rasheed are getting to know each other."

"I'm trying to like him, he seems like an alright guy." Brett wasn't sure where this was going but it wasn't what he wanted to talk about.

"He's a great guy. You should really take time to find out more about him." She had started rolling so she kept going, "Do you know why he is here in the US?"

"To go to school and play soccer I guess," Brett sounded a bit annoyed. What difference does it make he thought?

"I've sat and talked to him and his Aunt Maryam..." Before she could finish, Brett interrupted.

"Are you going out with him?" Jealousy rang through his words.

"No!" Madison was immediately defensive. "Just because I had a conversation with some guy, doesn't mean we are going out." She put finger quotes around her last words. "We went for pizza, I wanted to find out about him and his country." She didn't like having to defend her actions. "He took me to see his Aunt. She is an amazing lady, she's been all over the world and seen so many things. She's helping me."

Brett had tuned out most of her narration until the end, "Helping? With what?"

"Deciding what to do next year." Her answer caught him completely off guard.

"What do you mean? I thought you were still planning to go to Syracuse with me. You know the scouts were at the game. Coach thinks my chances are really good. That's what we both planned on, right?"

"That's really great Brett. I know that a scholarship has been your dream for so long." She sounded sincere and sad all at the same time. "But things are changing for me. I don't know what path I am going to take."

Brett was shocked. They had talked for two years about going to college together and it was still part of his major plans. "What about vet school?" He was pulling what he thought was his trump card.

"I'm just not sure anymore." She looked him squarely in the eyes, "Like you said, senior year isn't turning out like we planned. So much has changed." She got up and headed toward the house.

"Hey, wait." Brett called after her, "how about I come by the stable?"

She stopped and thought for a moment. "I don't think so, and...talk to Rasheed...about...something besides marshmallows."

Brett had no idea what she was talking about. All he knew is he had gone from being on top of the highest mountain peak to being in the bottom of the deepest, darkest cavern all in one night. He didn't understand how that could've happened.

CHAPTER 12

As Brett pulled into the Allendale campus on Monday he was surprised to see the courtyard strewn with blue and white streamers. A huge congratulatory banner, surrounded with balloons hung over the entrance. It lifted his spirits ever so slightly, but he was still bouncing between enthusiasm and grief since Friday night's happenings.

He pretended cheerfulness as fellow students yelled at him across the quad. Brett moved rapidly, so not to be caught in a conversation that he would have to completely fake. Entering American Government, the huddle of students broke into applauds. Heat raced from his toes to the top of his head, as he turned a brilliant shade of red. Offering a brief smile, he put his head down and headed for his normal seat in the back corner.

An equally rambunctious roar went up when Rasheed walked into the class. He smiled from ear to ear and searched for Brett. The bell rang before locating his target, so he headed for his usual front seat. He politely nodded his head in gratitude as classmates offered him kudos.

The students settled down as Ms. Michaels entered the class, dropping her load on the podium.

"Well, we definitely have some soccer stars in our midst!" The class let out hoots and howlers. "Let me offer my congratulations on a well-earned victory to all of you. It's very exciting that you're headed to the state championship. It's not ever occurred here at Allendale that I know of," she added.

She let the class enjoy the excitement for a few minutes longer. Brett could hear the enthusiasm travel from class to class down the hall. He wasn't feeling it!

"All right," Ms. Michaels wanted to get down to business, so taking her cue the students quieted. "Take out your human rights booklets, I want to finish up the last few articles." There was a shuffling of papers as everyone flipped through their notebooks and pulled out their pamphlets.

"I really want to focus on article 29 and what it means to each of you. Maddie, can you read point one aloud." That was out of the ordinary, so obviously Ms. Michaels was driving at something.

Madison started, "Everyone has duties to the community in which alone the free and full development of his personality is possible." The class sat quietly as she finished reading.

The sound of the ticking clock filled the silence. Ms. Michaels let the point soak in. Finally, she dropped the question, "In light of all the discussion we've had regarding human rights, what does this particular article mean to you?"

Madison's hand shot up like a rocket. Since the rest of the class still seemed to be pondering the implications, Ms. Michaels motioned to Maddie.

It was like taking the lid off of a pop-up snake can, Madison erupted with a fervor Brett had never witnessed.

"We all live such a sheltered life. I, for one, have never experienced any of the atrocities of discrimination or abuse that we have studied. Our parents have kept us in this perfect world, directing us toward a perfect future, where nothing bad would ever happen. Studying this unit, I've realized that I don't want to live inside that box, I want to take responsibility for the future of our planet and the rest of mankind. Like the article says, it's a duty."

Brett heard the passion in every word Madison spoke, she had undergone some kind of transformation.

"I don't mean any disrespect," she turned and caught Brett's attention, "Jessica was so brave and..." she stopped and choked on her words, "I hope I can find the courage to go out and make a change in the world with the abilities I have."

Brett was stunned. This must be what she was talking about after the game. He'd been so mixed up in his own issues over the past months that he hadn't taken time to notice what was going on in her world.

The class was soon caught up in a hot debate. Some agreed with Maddie, others felt living a successful life, doing what they wanted did fulfill their duty to the community.

Brett didn't hear their words. He was overwhelmed thinking about Madison going to the other side of the world. Is that what she intends? He couldn't let her do it. He couldn't be responsible for the loss of another person he loved. He had to somehow keep her from harm's way.

The bell ended the class deliberation. It jarred Brett from his thoughts. He had to get to Maddie before she headed out the door and was lost in the boisterous class change. But she jumped from her chair and made a beeline to Ms. Michaels. Within seconds, they were caught up in an intense conversation. It reminded Brett of the life-changing dialogue Jessica had at church last spring with Ms. Rodriguez. What is happening, Brett wondered. Standing at the door fidgeting with his books and watching the pandemonium in the hall, he tried to think of what he could say to Madison. What is she planning? Glancing at his watch, he realized he was going to be late for his next class. He shot one last look at the two conspiring about...who knows? That conversation is not ending any time soon, he thought. Dashing off down the hall, a new kind of dread crept into his world.

#####

Brett didn't feel any relief even as he headed for the soccer field after class. Looking out over the hiking trails he noticed everything had turned gray; the ground, the trees, the sky, they all matched his mood.

Stepping on the field, where only a handful of players were huddled, Brett realized everything was changing. The other fall sports had wound down so the athletic complex was deserted. Everyone had taken to the warmth of the gyms for the winter sport season.

"Hey Brett!" Coached snapped him out of this daze. He saw the team getting started on their warm-up of ball touches. Dropping his bag on a bench he trotted off toward the small group in the center of the field.

Running drills and mixing it up with his teammates cleared his mind for the most part, but he constantly felt a step behind where he should be. His mind was distracted. He became more and more frustrated as practice continued.

Finally, Coach Bronson chased the team off the field. As they headed for the lockers, Brett heard his coach call his name.

He stopped in his tracks. Did he really want to have this conversation? "Yeah," he turned slowly.

"You seemed a bit off in practice. You still having lady problems?" Coach didn't waste any time getting to the point.

"Yes...no...well, maybe," he stuttered. Brett felt the confusion tumbling around in his head. "It's about Maddie. I think she wants to go off and save the world." He felt a little ridiculous putting it so bluntly. "I'm not sure what she has going on, but it seems like this unit in American Government has changed the plans we had for the future. I'm afraid she is going to go off to the other side of the world, then..." he couldn't bring himself to finish his thought out loud.

"Like Jessica?" Coach knew exactly what was going on in his head.

"Why is it that they have to take on the problems of the world? I don't get it."

"They are both young ladies with passionate hearts. They want to help and feel like they're making a difference."

Brett shook his head in agreement, "That's for sure." He paused thinking over Coach's last words. "Do you feel like you make a difference Coach?"

"Well, every day I get to help young people move toward being responsible adults."

"But you just coach soccer." Brett considered his words.

"Is that really all I do?" He left the question hanging while Brett mulled it over. Coach saw it on Brett's face when the pieces of the puzzle clicked together.

"Oh...." A new respect for his coach washed over Brett.

"You see Brett, for me there is nothing more rewarding then watching a young person grow personally and take on the challenges of the world. I guess you could say that's what fulfills me. Everyone has to find that thing that makes them grow as a person. As long as you are helping others, then you're helping yourself move toward being a better person and creating a better world."

"But I just want to play soccer. How is that helping people?" Brett felt his brain creaking, as he tried to make sense of it all.

"That's OK for now, you'll figure it out."

"I just don't know how to protect Maddie." He failed to hide the worry in his voice.

"Talk to her. Tell her your concerns. More communication is better than less."

"Ok coach." Brett realized that he hadn't had a heart to heart with her since Jessica died.

"But, for now, I need you to do something for me." Brett perked his ears wondering how he could help his coach.

"We have one week, I need you to put this all aside and focus on soccer. The team needs your head in the game. The scouts will be there. Just one week...focus, OK?"

"Got it, I can do that." He felt relief wash over him as he formulated a plan. Heading toward the lockers, he stopped and turned as a realization hit him. "Coach, you and Gramps would have gotten along great!"

"I'm sure we would have!" Coach beamed.

#####

Brett got through the week doing exactly what his coach had asked, putting all his effort and energy into finishing out the season the best he could. The whole school was on an all-time high. Excitement rang through the halls as the week moved toward the State game. Brett couldn't walk down the hall without being barraged by encouragements and revelry. The hoopla rang through every bone in his body. Even Maddie had become engrossed in the pre-game buzz and was talking to him again.

The bedroom was dark and dismal when Brett's alarm went off Friday morning. Drawing his blinds, he saw that rain was coming down in buckets. This wasn't a good omen. Geez, he thought, I wonder what's going to happen if this doesn't let up.

The rain was still coming down in torrents by the time he reached school. The storm was the topic of conversation throughout the morning. Tension was high, it would be a horrible let down if the game were postponed or worse...cancelled. Brett tried to stay positive, it seemed to him that his whole life was riding on this game, he needed this chance.

During lunch a general announcement was aired that the weather front was moving on and the game was a go. Cheers reverberated through the entire school, the craze was back on. Brett felt relief course through his bones. At the final bell, the anticipation over the game was about to bust out of every pore of his body.

Coach planned a pregame dinner for the team, so they all gathered in the cafeteria at five. By 5:15 they were settling to a full on spread of every food a teenage boy loved.

"Hey, where's Rasheed?" His absence was alarming.

"He'll be here," Coach replied trying not to show any concern. The team continued to eat and chatter about the upcoming event. Their nerves subdued their excitement.

Coach slipped off and tried to call Rasheed but got no answer. He continued to reassure the rest of the team that all was fine. Brett knew something was up but made every effort to stay focused and positive about the game.

There was still no Rasheed by the time they were ready to board the bus. An unspoken concern punctuated every player's face.

Rasheed, Rasheed, what is happening, thought Brett. You know how important this game is to us. Maybe he'll show up at the stadium, he thought, trying to keep hope alive.

A cold drizzle started during warm-ups. This wasn't turning out to be the perfect night Brett had envisioned.

He did a quick once over of the stands. The crowd, huddled beneath their umbrellas and wrapped in parkas, were bundled together like sardines in a can. He finally spotted the scouts peering out from under a Syracuse parasol. Well, at least they showed up for the game, he thought.

Running out onto the field, Brett sensed the hole in the Allendale lineup. Standing across from the Lake Placid players, he felt miniaturized. Every player looked bigger and stronger than anyone on the Wolves team. It was intimidation at its max.

Allendale lost the toss, Lake Placid had the kick off. The whole game went downhill from there. Beside the field being wet and slippery, without Rasheed the team never seemed to get in sync. They struggled to take possession of the ball, much less to mount any offense. The Allendale stands were silent. The air had been let out of their swelled pride.

By half time the score was 3-0, Brett was fuming. Rasheed is going to have to answer to this, he thought as they headed toward the locker room. The team spent the fifteen minutes trying to warm their chilled bones and pretending they were going to get back in the game.

Trotting back onto the field, there was still a mist in the air. There couldn't have been a worse night for a game. The stands were now only half full, so it took

Brett only a few minutes to realize the Syracuse umbrella was gone.

He was overcome by despair. In Brett's mind, his whole future had been washed away in the rain. His torrent of emotions needed a target. There's only person to blame, Rasheed!

At the final whistle the score was 5-0. What an embarrassment! To Brett the whole season was a loss. How did they ever earn the right to be on the field for a shot at the State Championship? They left the field looking like whipped dogs. The sound of the celebrating Lake Placid players added insult to injury.

Climbing on the bus, the Allendale team was soaked to the bones. Their spirits were as drab as their bodies. The ride to the game had been filled with hope. Now riding home, they were numb.

Tucked in the corner of a back seat, all Brett could think of was how he was going to let Rasheed have it. Why did I ever trust him, he thought? I tried to like him. I tried to be his friend. This is what he did to me. Brett couldn't get any lower. He made a resolve.

Stepping off the bus, he didn't say a thing to any of the fans that had gathered to cheer them home. There is no reason to celebrate, he thought, pushing past the crowd.

"Brett." He heard Maddie's voice as he headed for his car. He ignored her plea. No one was stopping him now. He was headed to have it out with Rasheed!

CHAPTER 13

Brett swung his car into the drive where he knew Rasheed lived. The house was completely dark, but nothing was going to stop him now.

BAM, BAM, BAM....he understood the Hulk's strength fueled by rage. With wild fury he continued to pound...BAM, BAM, BAM, feeling like he could break down the door.

Within a few moments, lights slowly came on in the house. A rattling at the lock, then Aunt Maryam peering out of the chained crack.

"Brett, what's happening?" There was calm in her voice.

"Where is he? I need to see him...now!" His rage tipping on insanity.

"Brett, I don't really think Rasheed can speak with you right now." Concern crept into her tone.

"I...HAVE...TO...SEE...HIM...NOW!"

Aunt Maryam shrunk back from the outburst. Peering between the crack, Brett saw Rasheed appear around the corner.

"It's OK Aunt Maryam, he deserves an explanation." Rasheed was visibly shaken.

Aunt Maryam closed the door. Following another brief rattle, she opened it to Brett's boiling temper. Barging through the threshold, he zeroed in on Rasheed's somber expression. Reeling back, he balled his fist to deliver a mighty punch. Before his arm uncoiled, Rasheed looked him square in the eyes.

"My little sister was killed by a car bomber today."

Brett halted mid-action, he felt like he had just been sucker punched right in the gut!

Every emotion he had been fighting to contain since Jessica died, was unleashed in full hysteria. Before he could crumple to the floor, Aunt Maryam grabbed him on one side, Rasheed on the other. Together they escorted him to the couch in the dimly lit living room.

Rasheed sat beside him and wrapped his arm around Brett's slumped shoulders, as his Aunt had done for him only a few short hours before. It seemed like an eternity before Brett had exhausted his tears. When he finally lifted his head from his hands, Aunt Maryam was standing there with a warm washcloth and hot tea. He graciously accepted.

Forgetting his rage, he studied Rasheed's face, "What happened?"

"She had gone with my mother to the market. Father said they were walking through the plaza when an old car squealed to a halt in the middle of the road. Witnesses said, seconds later it exploded."

"Your mother? Is she alright?" Brett didn't know he could feel this much pain.

"She was injured but will be fine. My sister was hit by flying debris that..." Rasheed stopped mid-sentence as tears rolled down his cheek.

There was silence for a few minutes as Rasheed tried to contain himself.

"I have no words to console you. I'm so sorry." Brett felt every bit of Rasheed's grief.

As both of them tried to gather their emotions, Aunt Maryam bustled around bringing tissues, blankets and more tea. Finally, after they were settled she spoke.

"Brett, Maddie has told me your sister was in Afghanistan, what happened there?" Brett was sucked in by the kindness and concern in her voice. The whole story spilled out in a torrent, from his part in convincing their parents to let her go, to the day she died. Aunt Maryam sat quietly listening, encouraging him to continue through the rough parts.

"I see, what else?" She paused looking at him with pure compassion.

Studying her face, he rolled the question around trying to unravel the last of his emotions. Finally, he voiced what Maddie had nudged at weeks ago, "I should have stopped her. I got so caught up in her excitement, it's all my fault that she died."

"Brett, you knew your sister well?"

"Very..."

"Do you think you could have stopped her once she made up her mind?" That was something Brett had never considered.

"Probably not," he chuckled, remembering Jessica's determination in life.

"Brett, it was never your fault. Just as it wasn't Rasheed's fault that he wasn't there for his little sister today. There are some bad people in this world and unfortunately both of your sisters were in their path at the wrong time. Nothing either of you could have done would have changed that instant."

GINGER RODEGHERO

Brett pondered that for a bit, shaking his head in agreement. "You're probably right but...the pain is unbearable. I've never felt this helpless. I don't know how I will ever learn to live with my decision."

"I have that same feeling," Rasheed added.

Aunt Maryam glanced between the two of them. "Some people wear their pain like a mantle for everyone to see, but most people bury it deep in their heart afraid that if it were brought to light, it would break them. The way to live with your misfortune is to confront your decisions of the past. Know that any choices you made, at that moment in time, was the best decision you could have made with the information you had. Learn from that experience and move forward to create a future."

Aunt Maryam's wisdom jarred Brett out of his grief. Looking at Rasheed, he thought of Maddie's decision for a gap year. Then he remembered something else Maddie said.

Turning to Rasheed, he asked, "Why are you here in America?"

Rasheed paused, something had changed between them in the last hour. It was time to share his story. Taking a deep breath, he began.

"My country has a long history of war-torn strife. There are many factions, each headed by a drug lord that uses medieval methods to scare the people into cooperation. My father is a very important man, with a very important job to repair the dam that will provide water to the Helmand Valley. He is also a very brave man. A particularly evil warlord came to him demanding money. Baba stood up to him and refused to submit to his demands."

"So, what does that have to do with you being here?" Brett's curiosity was getting the best of him.

"Mullah Sharif Anis," Rasheed continued, "I will never forget this man. He was very insulted and he threatened my father. We were all so concerned about something happening to Baba, that we did not consider the safety of the rest of the family. One day, when I was running to the market for my mother, I was kidnapped. I was held captive in a small closet-sized room with a dirt floor for about a month."

"I can't imagine," Brett wondered how Rasheed survived. "Was it this Mullah guy that took you?"

"Yes, but there is more." Summoning all of his courage, Rasheed continued. "He used me for his personal, perverted pleasure." Rasheed spat the words out like a snake spitting venom.

"You mean..." Brett couldn't think of the words to continue.

"He raped me...many times." Rasheed studied Brett's face for any reaction.

Stunned, Brett did not know how to react. Finally, grabbing Rasheed, placing forehead to forehead, he whispered the only words he could summon. "I'm so, so sorry you experienced that."

The moment that passed between them sealed a bond that would never be broken.

But Brett wanted the rest of the story, "How did you get away?"

For Rasheed, the hard part was over so he plunged forward, "Mullah was demanding money for my release. I didn't know what my father would do, but as I said he is very important. He was able to get government assistance, they raided the compound where I was being held and rescued me. I remember the relief in my father's face when he saw that I was still alive."

"So, you are here because your dad didn't want it to happen again?" Brett wanted to fit the last pieces of the story together.

"No, I did not want to leave my family, but I was suffering from what you Americans would call PTSD. I had very bad dreams, I couldn't eat, I feared to leave my house. Finally, my mother insisted I needed to get out of the environment that reminded me of my suffering. They sent me here to live with Aunt Maryam. It was very hard to do, but Aunt Maryam has been very gracious and understanding. And there has been soccer!"

Brett saw the affectionate exchange between them, he felt the same tenderness for this woman. She was not as fragile as she looked.

In the quiet of the room, Brett sensed a calm he had not ever experienced before. His earlier anger had melted into a new resolve. There were things he had to handle in his life to move on, the first one being Maddie.

Aunt Maryam interrupted his thoughts, "Brett, it's late. Your mother will be concerned."

"You're right, I should go." He paused, blushing. "I really should apologize for my earlier behavior."

"There is no need," Rasheed offered his fist, "I probably would have reacted the same."

Brett smiled in relief as their fists met. "Thanks, brother!"

#####

Brett woke in his crumpled bed still in his jeans and t-shirt. Peering outside it looked as if a cloud had fallen to the earth. His brain was immersed in the same kind of fog. It only took a brief moment for him to clear his thoughts and recall his resolve of the night before. He had to see Maddie.

Before he even reached for his phone, a ping, followed by her smiling face appeared on the screen. Hand shaking, he opened the text.

"I'm at the stable"

He felt a rush of relief. It sounded like an invite to him. The first in weeks.

He took the steps downstairs, two at a time, but stopped short when he saw his mom standing in the kitchen. Concern written all over her face.

"What happened to you after the game?" She tried to control the quiver in her voice.

He had Maddie on his mind, but knew his mother deserved an explanation. He grabbed her hands and led her to the table. Sitting down beside her, he realized that she needed to know he was going to be OK.

"Mom, I didn't mean to worry you last night." He paused thinking she might jump into a well-deserved admonishment for causing her such concern.

"I was really upset after we lost and I blamed it on Rasheed. So, I went to his house to have it out with him." Beginning to explain, the calm and resolve from the previous night returned. Something had changed in his world.

"What happened to Rasheed?" He heard her motherly concern, even for this boy she knew little of.

"Mom, please, I don't want to upset you." Brett somehow felt responsible for how his mother may react to the news he was about to share.

"Brett, tell me what happened." Her eyes studied Brett's face searching for the answer.

"Rasheed's little sister was killed by a car bomb yesterday." He sat waiting, wondering how the news would hit her.

Tears rolled down her cheeks. Her hands trembled. Brett stood and wrapped his arms around her. No words were needed, he knew exactly what she was going through.

#####

By the time he finally left for the stable, the sun was beginning to burn off the fog. Brett tried to gather his thoughts, exactly what did he need to say to Maddie. He recalled Aunt Maryam's words, learn from your experience.

The parking lot was almost empty, so he pulled up to the stable door hoping to avoid the sea of puddles created by yesterday's storm. Bruno was sitting at his post, almost as if he was expecting Brett to show up. He walked quietly beside Brett down the aisle toward

Midnight's home. Brett was happy for the moral support.

"Hello," he said softly as he peered into the stall.

Maddie stopped instantly, put down her brush and rushed to Brett. Wrapping her arms around him, they stood quietly together.

Maddie finally broke the silence, "I was so worried about you."

"The feeling is mutual," Brett whispered.

"Where did you tear off to last night? Everyone was concerned. I sent text after text. It was a long night." Brett could see that he had caused her distress.

"I'm sorry. But it was time I needed," he wanted to explain it all but he needed to say his piece. "I can't let you go off to Afghanistan like Jess did."

Maddie was shocked, "What do you mean?"

"I know you need to go help people. But please, you can't go there."

"Brett, I don't plan to go there. What gave you that idea?" She was confused but touched by his concern.

"You, in class, talking about helping people. Then after class with Ms. Michaels. You can't go there, please." He sounded like he was begging but he didn't care.

"Brett, I don't plan to go to Afghanistan." As she repeated those words, relief washed over him.

"Then...what?" Brett had to know she would be safe.

"Ms. Michaels has been helping me with research. There are many organizations...here in the US." Her eyes locked with his. "Where people can help. I have been looking at Thorn. It was started by Ashton Kutcher to help protect children from sexual exploitation. There are many other organizations that help people who have been rescued from human trafficking. I'm still looking to see where I can best use my abilities. I've come to realize that we are all one mankind and I need to do something for those who suffer. I have the rest of this year to decide how and where. I want to take a gap year and..." she paused. "I just need to help."

The strain melted off his shoulders, "OK Maddie. I understand. I just need to be sure you're going to be safe."

"Brett, anything can happen, any day, to anyone. We just need to make the best of each day we have been given." In that moment, Brett felt more love for Maddie than he had ever had before. Pulling her tightly to his chest, he inhaled deeply, trying to hold onto that moment forever.

"Wait Brett," she looked up into his baby blues. "Where did you go last night?"

"To beat up Rasheed," he laughed.

"What?"

Before she could say more, he sat her down to explain. "I was really upset that he didn't come to the game."

"Yeah, we all got that! What happened?"

"Rasheed's little sister was killed." There was no other way to put it.

Maddie was speechless and obviously stunned.

"A car bomber, she was hit by stray debris."

"Poor Rasheed," then she stopped. "Oh Brett, I'm so sorry you had to be reminded, well you know…of Jess."

"Yeah, it was an interesting night, but I'm good."

"Tell me Brett," the tenderness in her voice reminded him of the two other ladies he had spoken with in the last twelve hours. I'm so fortunate to have this many people who care for me, he thought.

"Aunt Maryam happened!" Brett smiled.

Maddie nodded, knowing exactly what he meant. They sat in the hay alongside Midnight, Bruno snuggled between them, for over an hour. Brett told Maddie the whole story. Tears rolled down her face as he reiterated the story of Rasheed's kidnapping.

"He is such a sweet, gentle guy, even after all that." Brett understood her feelings for Rasheed.

"But, he has the best thing in the world to help him get through," he noted.

"What's that?" Maddie was puzzled, trying to figure out what he was getting at.

"Aunt Maryam!"

"Oh yeah, Aunt Maryam," Maddie flashed her beautiful smile.

CHAPTER 14

The cloud hanging over the school on Monday morning reflected the mood of the whole student body. In comparison to the excitement last Friday, the halls were as somber as a dirge. No one dared mention the results of the game, the bitter loss was still too fresh in their minds.

The news of Rasheed's sister had run through the school like a wildfire on a prairie. The tragedy had hit too close to home. Brett's friends tiptoed around any conversation that would bring either topic to the forefront.

Brett thought about Rasheed almost every moment of every day, wondering how he was doing, feeling the pain he knew he was going through. Madison stuck close to Brett through the week watching for any signs that he might crack, ready to step in if need be.

By Friday, the school atmosphere was getting back to normal. The talk at the lunch table was about the season's opening basketball game against Bloomfield. Brett was quietly listening to the chatter when he felt a tap on his shoulder and was handed a note. Briefly glancing at the paper, he stuffed it in his pocket.

"What's up?" asked Kaleb.

Madison shot him that "look," trying to get Kaleb to keep the conversation upbeat.

"It's OK," said Brett, noticing the effort. "Coach wants to see me after lunch. Really guys, it's OK. Please stop treating me like I might break. It's been a tough week, but deep down I'm doing better than I have since Jessica died."

Everyone around the table was staring at him in wonder. He hadn't ever been this relaxed or outspoken about Jessica and they weren't sure how to react.

Brett scanned the faces around the table, he could see the bewilderment in their eyes.

"I've come to peace with Jessica's death. Bad things happen. I can't stop living my life. Really, my concern is for Rasheed now. If there is anyone who needs our help and understanding, it's him." He saw the heads quietly bob in agreement.

The silence at the table was interrupted by the bell. One by one, his friends came and gave him a hug. The other students in the cafeteria watched in silence, wondering what had occurred.

Brett made his way through the halls to the athletic office. He stopped short when he saw the back of a head sitting in a chair across from Coach Bronson. They were deep in conversation and Brett could see the empathy on Coach's face. Should I wait or knock he wondered.

Instantly, as if there had been a thought transference, Coach looked up and waved to him to come in. Opening the door and stepping in he saw the other student in the room was Rasheed. He rushed straight to him and grabbed him in a bear hug.

"Hey man, how are you doing?" Brett stared him straight in the face trying to look into his soul.

"I'm getting by." Rasheed remained composed. Coach excused himself and stepped out letting the two have a private conversation.

"You're all I've thought about this week," Brett began. "I wanted to come to see you, but didn't know your customs. I remembered I didn't want to talk to people," Brett felt like he was rambling. "Are you ok?"

"There was a service for my sister, Wednesday. I wished I were there. But my mom is coming soon. We will have a service here so I can put my grief to rest. In the meantime, well, you know…I have…"

"Aunt Maryam," they said in unison.

Coach tapped lightly on the door, "Can I join this conversation now?"

"Sure Coach, thanks for bringing Rasheed here. I really needed to see him." Brett felt relief wash over him.

"Well, it really wasn't me that orchestrated this meeting. Just a minute." Coach left the room. Rasheed and Brett looked at each other, wondering what that was all about.

Minutes later, he returned followed by the Syracuse scout, Mr. Wells. Coach stepped aside and let him have the floor.

"I drove down here to talk to you two not knowing what had happened. But your coach said we should go ahead and talk. First, Rasheed, please let me offer my sincere condolences for your loss." Mr. Wells said with all sincerity.

"Thank you, sir." Rasheed bowed humbly. "But please, tell us what has brought you here?"

"I have enjoyed watching you two on the soccer field this year. You have both grown as players and make an amazing duo." He paused briefly, looking to see if either of them were onto him yet. "I drove down here personally, because I would like to offer both of you a full ride scholarship to Syracuse next year. I think together, you two would be a great addition to our squad."

Brett and Rasheed stood staring, as if shell shocked. The seconds ticked by before either of them could speak, Coach Bronson blurted out, "WELL?"

The two players looked at each other, Rasheed stuck out his fist. A huge smile broke over both of their faces. As their fists came together, they agreed, "Let's do this!"

Around the room, hands were shook. There was a new future in the air.

"I will meet with you and your parents in a few weeks. We will go over all the details. Until then, congratulations on a great season." Mr. Wells left the players with their coach.

"Brett, can I have one more minute before you go back to class?" Coach Bronson had something else on his mind.

"I'll talk to you later Rasheed." Both teens stopped for a moment and exchanged one more fist bump.

"Yeah, later." Rasheed's mood seemed to have lifted.

"Coach, what else do you need from me?" Brett was curious as to what he had brewing.

"Brett, the junior rec teams are organizing for the spring season. I was wondering if you would be interested in helping out with a youth team. You have great potential for coaching and I think the kids would love you."

Brett didn't need to think about it, "I'd love to! I want those kids to love the sport as much as I do!"

"Great, I'll get you the info." Coach Bronson knew this was a good path for Brett. "Now, you need to get back to class."

Brett headed for the door but paused and walked back across the room. "Coach, thanks for everything you've done for me...and for Rasheed. I wouldn't have made it through this season without you." Brett turned and headed for the door.

"Hey, Brett."

"Yeah Coach." Brett looked back, wondering what else he could want.

"That's why I do this!"

Brett completely understood.

#####

Brett floated through the rest of his classes. This is what he had wanted for so long, finally something was going his way. When the final bell rang, he headed straight for his car without stopping. He still had one thing he needed to do.

He didn't have to think as he pulled his car from the school lot, he was headed for the cemetery. It was time to lay this tragedy to rest.

The late day sun was shining through the now bare trees. He headed through the forest, down the nature trail to Jessica's resting place. The sun's rays were reflecting off the bronze memorial stone, shining as brightly as Jessica always had.

"Hi Jess, so much has happened. I wish you were here, sitting on the couch with your feet across my lap. I would tell you everything." He paused, "I remember how you loved me to massage your toes." A calm smile lit his face as he reminisced.

"I'm going to Syracuse to play soccer, like I always planned. I hope you are proud of me. But to be honest, I don't think I would have been offered the scholarship without Rasheed. He made me a better player." Brett thought that over for just a moment. "No, Jessica... Rasheed made me a better person."

Brett sat by Jessica's memorial stone and told her Rasheed's story. By the time the sun was setting behind the trees, he had finished.

"One more thing, Jess. I am so proud of you. I understand why you went to Afghanistan and your need to help. Your life made a difference. I am going to live mine so you will be proud of me. I love you so much. I will hold you in my heart forever."

Brett felt at peace as he strolled back to his car. Life was lighter somehow. Pulling into the drive at home, he saw his mom getting out of her car.

"Hey mom, do you need any help?"

"No, I'm good." Brett noticed that his mother seemed more tranquil. "I went to visit Rasheed's Aunt today."

"Great!" Brett replied, that explained everything. Aunt Maryam had worked her magic!

REFERENCES

The Universal Declaration was adopted by the General
Assembly of the United Nations on 10 December 1948.
Motivated by the experiences of the preceding world
wars, the Universal Declaration was the first time that
countries agreed on a comprehensive statement of
inalienable human rights.

The Universal Declaration begins by recognizing that
'the inherent dignity of all members of the human
family is the foundation of freedom, justice and peace
in the world'.

It declares that human rights are universal − to be
enjoyed by all people, no matter who they are or where
they live.

The Universal Declaration includes civil and political rights, like the right to life, liberty, free speech and privacy. It also includes economic, social and cultural rights, like the right to social security, health and education.

(Source:https://www.humanrights.gov.au/our-work/what-universal-declaration-human-rights)

UNIVERSAL DECLARATION OF HUMAN RIGHTS

(Source:https://en.wikisource.org/wiki/Universal_Declaration_of_Human_Rights)

Whereas recognition of the inherent dignity and of the equal and inalienable rights of all members of the human family is the foundation of freedom, justice and peace in the world,

Whereas disregard and contempt for human rights have resulted in barbarous acts which have outraged the conscience of mankind, and the advent of a world in which human beings shall enjoy freedom of speech and belief and freedom from fear and want has been proclaimed as the highest aspiration of the common people,

Whereas it is essential, if man is not to be compelled to have recourse, as a last resort, to rebellion against tyranny and oppression, that human rights should be protected by the rule of law,

Whereas it is essential to promote the development of friendly relations between nations,

Whereas the peoples of the United Nations have in the Charter reaffirmed their faith in fundamental human rights, in the dignity and worth of the human person and in the equal rights of men and women and have determined to promote social progress and better standards of life in larger freedom,

Whereas Member States have pledged themselves to achieve, in co-operation with the United Nations, the promotion of universal respect for and observance of human rights and fundamental freedoms,

Whereas a common understanding of these rights and freedoms is of the greatest importance for the full realization of this pledge,

Now, Therefore THE GENERAL ASSEMBLY proclaims THIS UNIVERSAL DECLARATION OF HUMAN RIGHTS as a common standard of achievement for all peoples and all nations, to the end that every individual and every organ of society, keeping this Declaration constantly in mind, shall strive by teaching and education to promote respect for these rights and freedoms and by progressive measures, national and international, to secure their universal and effective recognition and observance, both among the peoples of Member States themselves and among the peoples of territories under their jurisdiction.

Article 1.
All human beings are born free and equal in dignity and rights. They are endowed with reason and conscience and should act towards one another in a spirit of brotherhood.

Article 2.
Everyone is entitled to all the rights and freedoms set forth in this Declaration, without distinction of any kind, such as race, colour, sex, language, religion, political or other opinion, national or social origin, property, birth or other status. Furthermore, no distinction shall be made on the basis of the political, jurisdictional or international status of the country or territory to which a person belongs, whether it be independent, trust, non-self-governing or under any other limitation of sovereignty.

Article 3.
Everyone has the right to life, liberty and security of person.

Article 4.
No one shall be held in slavery or servitude; slavery and the slave trade shall be prohibited in all their forms.

Article 5.
No one shall be subjected to torture or to cruel,

inhuman or degrading treatment or punishment.

Article 6.
Everyone has the right to recognition everywhere as a person before the law.

Article 7.
All are equal before the law and are entitled without any discrimination to equal protection of the law. All are entitled to equal protection against any discrimination in violation of this Declaration and against any incitement to such discrimination.

Article 8.
Everyone has the right to an effective remedy by the competent national tribunals for acts violating the fundamental rights granted him by the constitution or by law.

Article 9.
No one shall be subjected to arbitrary arrest, detention or exile.

Article 10.
Everyone is entitled in full equality to a fair and public hearing by an independent and impartial tribunal, in the determination of his rights and obligations and of any criminal charge against him.

Article 11.

(1) Everyone charged with a penal offence has the right to be presumed innocent until proved guilty according to law in a public trial at which he has had all the guarantees necessary for his defense.

(2) No one shall be held guilty of any penal offence on account of any act or omission which did not constitute a penal offence, under national or international law, at the time when it was committed. Nor shall a heavier penalty be imposed than the one that was applicable at the time the penal offence was committed.

Article 12.

No one shall be subjected to arbitrary interference with his privacy, family, home or correspondence, nor to attacks upon his honour and reputation. Everyone has the right to the protection of the law against such interference or attacks.

Article 13.

(1) Everyone has the right to freedom of movement and residence within the borders of each state.

(2) Everyone has the right to leave any country, including his own, and to return to his country.

Article 14.

(1) Everyone has the right to seek and to enjoy in other countries asylum from persecution.

(2) This right may not be invoked in the case of prosecutions genuinely arising from non-political crimes

or from acts contrary to the purposes and principles of the United Nations.

Article 15.

(1) Everyone has the right to a nationality.

(2) No one shall be arbitrarily deprived of his nationality nor denied the right to change his nationality.

Article 16.

(1) Men and women of full age, without any limitation due to race, nationality or religion, have the right to marry and to found a family. They are entitled to equal rights as to marriage, during marriage and at its dissolution.

(2) Marriage shall be entered into only with the free and full consent of the intending spouses.

(3) The family is the natural and fundamental group unit of society and is entitled to protection by society and the State.

Article 17.

(1) Everyone has the right to own property alone as well as in association with others.

(2) No one shall be arbitrarily deprived of his property.

Article 18.

Everyone has the right to freedom of thought, conscience and religion; this right includes freedom to change his religion or belief, and freedom, either alone or in community with others and in public or private, to manifest his religion or belief in teaching, practice, worship and observance.

Article 19.

Everyone has the right to freedom of opinion and expression; this right includes freedom to hold opinions without interference and to seek, receive and impart information and ideas through any media and regardless of frontiers.

Article 20.

(1) Everyone has the right to freedom of peaceful assembly and association.
(2) No one may be compelled to belong to an association.

Article 21.

(1) Everyone has the right to take part in the government of his country, directly or through freely chosen representatives.
(2) Everyone has the right of equal access to public service in his country.
(3) The will of the people shall be the basis of the authority of government; this will shall be expressed in periodic and genuine elections which shall be by universal and equal suffrage and shall be held by secret vote or by equivalent free voting procedures.

Article 22.

Everyone, as a member of society, has the right to social security and is entitled to realization, through national effort and international co-operation and in accordance with the organization and resources of each State, of the economic, social and cultural rights indispensable for his dignity and the free development of his personality.

Article 23.

(1) Everyone has the right to work, to free choice of employment, to just and favourable conditions of work and to protection against unemployment.

(2) Everyone, without any discrimination, has the right to equal pay for equal work.

(3) Everyone who works has the right to just and favourable remuneration ensuring for himself and his family an existence worthy of human dignity, and supplemented, if necessary, by other means of social protection.

(4) Everyone has the right to form and to join trade unions for the protection of his interests.

Article 24.

Everyone has the right to rest and leisure, including reasonable limitation of working hours and periodic holidays with pay.

Article 25.

(1) Everyone has the right to a standard of living adequate for the health and well-being of himself and of his family, including food, clothing, housing and medical care and necessary social services, and the right to security in the event of unemployment, sickness, disability, widowhood, old age or other lack of livelihood in circumstances beyond his control.

(2) Motherhood and childhood are entitled to special care and assistance. All children, whether born in or out of wedlock, shall enjoy the same social protection.

Article 26.

(1) Everyone has the right to education. Education shall be free, at least in the elementary and fundamental stages. Elementary education shall be compulsory. Technical and professional education shall be made generally available and higher education shall be equally accessible to all on the basis of merit.

(2) Education shall be directed to the full development of the human personality and to the strengthening of respect for human rights and fundamental freedoms. It shall promote understanding, tolerance and friendship among all nations, racial or religious groups, and shall further the activities of the United Nations for the maintenance of peace.

(3) Parents have a prior right to choose the kind of education that shall be given to their children.

Article 27.

(1) Everyone has the right freely to participate in the cultural life of the community, to enjoy the arts and to share in scientific advancement and its benefits.

(2) Everyone has the right to the protection of the moral and material interests resulting from any scientific, literary or artistic production of which he is the author.

Article 28.

Everyone is entitled to a social and international order in which the rights and freedoms set forth in this Declaration can be fully realized.

Article 29.

(1) Everyone has duties to the community in which alone the free and full development of his personality is possible.

(2) In the exercise of his rights and freedoms, everyone shall be subject only to such limitations as are determined by law solely for the purpose of securing due recognition and respect for the rights and freedoms of others and of meeting the just requirements of morality, public order and the general welfare in a democratic society.

(3) These rights and freedoms may in no case be exercised contrary to the purposes and principles of the United Nations.

Article 30.

Nothing in this Declaration may be interpreted as implying for any State, group or person any right to engage in any activity or to perform any act aimed at the destruction of any of the rights and freedoms set forth herein.

ABOUT THE AUTHOR

My love of reading began as soon as I learned to decode letters. Reading voraciously, I learned how to write. My love for children guided me into the field of education. My desire to help others brought these two passions together. How can one look around the world and not want to change what they see? I write to communicate to the next generation in a way that they will hopefully strive to make our world a better place.